Basketball Guide

Basketball is One of the Utmost Challenging

(Greatest Players and Stories From the 2000 Era of Basketball)

William Smith

Published By **Andrew Zen**

William Smith

All Rights Reserved

Basketball Guide: Basketball is One of the Utmost Challenging (Greatest Players and Stories From the 2000 Era of Basketball)

ISBN 978-0-9950957-1-7

No part of this guidebook shall be reproduced in any form without permission in writing from the publisher except in the case of brief quotations embodied in critical articles or reviews.

Legal & Disclaimer

The information contained in this book is not designed to replace or take the place of any form of medicine or professional medical advice. The information in this book has been provided for educational & entertainment purposes only.

The information contained in this book has been compiled from sources deemed reliable, and it is accurate to the best of the Author's knowledge; however, the Author cannot guarantee its accuracy and validity and cannot be held liable for any errors or omissions. Changes are periodically made to this book. You must consult your doctor or get professional medical advice before using any of the suggested remedies, techniques, or information in this book.

Upon using the information contained in this book, you agree to hold harmless the Author from and against any damages, costs, and expenses, including any legal fees potentially resulting from the application of any of the information provided by this guide. This disclaimer applies to any damages or injury caused by the use and application, whether directly or indirectly, of any advice or information presented, whether for breach of contract, tort, negligence, personal injury, criminal intent, or under any other cause of action.

You agree to accept all risks of using the information presented inside this book. You need to consult a professional medical practitioner in order to ensure you are both able and healthy enough to participate in this program.

Table Of Contents

Chapter 1: Core Values 1

Chapter 2: Practice Management And Planning 12

Chapter 3: Skill Development.................. 24

Chapter 4: Motion Cutting Teaching Progression 44

Chapter 5: Progressive Teaching Plan 55

Chapter 6: The Rules Of Basketball 61

Chapter 7: Basketball For Beginners 74

Chapter 8: Basketball & Nba Betting...... 95

Chapter 9: Gathering Information........ 110

Chapter 10: Overvaluing Of The Most Popular Teams 128

Chapter 11: Letdowns & Bounce-Back Games.. 144

Chapter 12: Improve Your Basketball I.Q. 160

Chapter 13: Improve Your Shooting..... 172

Chapter 1: Core Values

Pete Carroll in his book Win Forever: Live, work, and play like A Champion, says "The simple act of making thoughtful, affirmative statements about who we are and what we want to achieve can be an incredibly powerful tool for getting the best possible performance out of ourselves." In addition, he says that if you change our identity every year, then it will be impossible to excel at what we do. As a coach for youth basketball, it's crucial you've got three to five values you've written down that you hold to with all your heart and can remain true to. These values are the basis of your team's community and influence an environment that encourages positive behavior in your group both in and out of the court. These values should be clear enough that everybody on your team is aware of who we are and is of importance for us. The current youth organization you are part of or your coaches at your high school may possess these principles clearly stated which they would like to teach and reinforced throughout the course of the season. It is possible that you will have to define the values on your own based upon your own personal beliefs about what is most crucial to the organization that you coach.

A few examples of teams that are successful in delineating their core values and implementing them are the American Military Academy West Point's primary values of honor, duty and nation, as well as the University of Virginia men's basketball team's values of humbleness as well as unity, passion, dedication and gratitude. Both teams have clarified who they are as well as what they would like to represent. They are a united group which guides their the way they conduct themselves in a positive direction. West Point is one of the top universities for leadership and Tony Bennett's squad is at University of Virginia has been one of the most successful basketball teams throughout the United States with a National Championship that was won in the year the year 2019.

It is possible that you are thinking it's just a matter of the fifth grade coach of a youth basketball team. This is not a college or professional school and this notion of core values is a bit over over the top. We fully understand that and human nature to believe this. By determining what fundamental values you would like to be emphasized and taught to your children, you are making a significant step towards being above the average, not an average team or even a program. This is a huge leap towards shaping your team and your child to be a positive influence in both the classroom and on the field.

In the case of youth basketball players between the ages of five and eight This could be saying to the group that we're emphasizing paying attention, working hard and having fun, and specifying what these values will are. We as coaches know our players are paying attention whenever they're not running around with the ball, or conversing with colleagues and keep their eyes fixed on you even when speaking. It is important to give the very best effort you can, and not making comparisons to the other team members. If we pay attention and put in the effort, we'll enjoy ourselves. When you have defined these values, Ask your team members whether they are in agreement so that they feel a sense ownership. Additionally, when you witness those core values being demonstrated, you should be able to praise these values in front of your audience.

Motivation

Daniel Coyle, in his book The Talent Code, does incredible work in examining motivation's many aspects that he calls ignition. He also explains how "Ignition supplies the energy, while deep practice translates that energy over time into forward progress." As as a coach, you'll contribute to generating the enthusiasm and motivation that your team members have to work to be better, work harder, and adhere to your team's fundamental principles. It is your job to be involved in setting the goals and what you want to achieve of your team. In this section, we'll explore how motivation is generated and sustained, as well as the reasons why commitment to long-term goals to language, physical surroundings are crucial. The chapter will also look at ways to increase intrinsic motivation as well as the best time to apply extrinsic motivation.

Long-Term Commitment

It's a tense to ask, however asking your child or the team the question, what length of time you'll be playing basketball for is vital. The options include this school year, through primary school, high school, as well as throughout my existence. It's important to inquire for a long-term commitment because people who have learned an idea from their environment which has led them to make a longer-term commitments have demonstrated significantly more improvement in performance when assessed compared to people who have quick-term commitment reactions. The importance of having fun and a lifetime involvement of basketball is crucial. It is important to have your child or team identify a character or group of people with whom they can identify with, and then letting them think, "I want to be like them or I want to be a part of this group," could be an extremely effective motivator to commit for the long haul. Everyone remembers the experience of a full gymnasium during tournaments and thinking about how enjoyable it was to participate in it. We've seen youngsters who manage the team of 18U and varsity develop into excellent athletes and join good teams once they reach the age of.

Language

As a coach for youth, the language we speak and the things that we communicate to our players at a very young stage are crucial regarding motivation and building confidence. Regarding giving praise, the players first need earned it. The effort of praise and the slow pace over natural talents or the results. We have a sense of the things we consider important. When we praise the talent of others or the results of these teams, they tend to steer clear of challenges or errors. If we praise efforts and slow progress, teams are more likely to be more focused to work hard, get involved and love advancing their capabilities. They're not scared to be embarrassed and enthusiastic about opportunities. One of the most important aspects to improve is being confident enough to make mistakes and experiencing the ability to compete. Competing with the best talents is something that should be celebrated since that's what will help your team improve.

Physical Environment

When safety concerns have been taken care of areas that are not attractive can send an indication that things aren't so great in the market and you need to get inspired right now. That's the main motivational sign of the scarcity. When our young players have a constant, pleasant atmosphere, they can inadvertently demotivate. This shouldn't be an issue for the majority of young basketball teams since prime gymnasium space and time are generally reserved by older teams. It is nevertheless important to be aware that, just like Rocky Balboa, training in gymnasiums with no filtration is a boon to increase motivation.

Intrinsic and Extrinsic Motivation

In a perfect world, our group would feel intrinsically motivated to play basketball and increase their skills levels. Basketball and enhancing their abilities at home would bring them joy and create a sense satisfaction versus feeling extrinsically driven to win or the outcome of a bad situation. But, that's not often the case.

Strategies to boost intrinsic motivation can be achieved by finding a role model that is positive or a an organization that you will identify with, which can help improve longer-term commitment. Also, praise the effort and efforts versus inherent abilities or results, establishing the clearest action plan or commitment agreement for developing skills that everyone in your team can have the right to approve and take is accountable for, and promoting cooperation and collaboration in your group. The commitment agreement should be posted at home so that the team members are able to see it every daily for a daily reminder. The goals may change over the year.

The best applications of extrinsic motivation occurs when level of skill is lacking and your group might not have a lot of interest for a specific task as well as for tasks that are routine like completing taking home five or 10 minute sheets of drills. Youth practices that are for kids aged nine to fourteen take place twice a week. We've found that offering an incentive of a modest amount (freeze pop small sports drinks, water bottle sticker) to complete homework drill sheets that require only five to 10 minutes during organized practice, goes far in the development of better ball handling abilities. When the fundamental skill level and the initial motivational factor has been achieved, external stimuli may be removed. They could be harmful for the long term, but they are in addition to basketball, and can lead to developing skills, which could feel like working or being a burden.

Chapter 2: Practice Management And Planning

Training and managing behavior is essential for improving as well as efficient training. An organized group can be able to remain focused and achieve more, which ultimately leads to more fun for everyone who are. This can be achieved by setting the minimum number of clearly defined rules for the first time routine for conduct, rewarding the moment a positive behaviour is displayed as well as having a strategy that is in place for the more challenging players. In any situation and especially at the young levels, the value and specifics of listening have to be made clear.

It is obvious that we are listening when we focus focused on our coach and there is no interruptions to discussions with our buddies, and there's no bounce of the ball, which displays respect, and can help us grow. As a youth coach, you should not give instruction until this attitude has been demonstrated. Eventually, the habit of listening will develop on behalf of your team. Also, it is important to show what hard work as well as being a team player takes (in the stance of a person, jumping onto the ground for loose balls, putting in the best of ourselves and encouraging the players) and to then cheer with joy as these traits can be observed.

There are times when you're dealing with players that struggle to meet this behavior expectation. They might be unable to pay attention and divert attention from others and may even say harmful remarks to teammates or have difficulty focusing. If you have a strategy to deal with these scenarios, you are able to make more informed decisions and avoid reactivity. It is recommended to first give the participant one or two reminders to the agreed-upon guidelines. If the player is not satisfied, it, have the player take during the session, and then have them be ready to return. Follow up with the practice with a post or prior discussion with your child about your and the players' concerns. A final step is a parent and player meeting. parent's meeting is a last step in case all other solutions did not work.

To ensure the most efficient and well-organized exercise, practicing planning is essential. Be a kid and plan to enjoy the future. It is easiest to do this by playing games that complement your skills practice, stressing effort and steady growth, while creating clear expectations for behavior in the past. Our preferred teaching method is to teach the skill and then play it. For example, the ball handling techniques that is followed by dribble tags or Dribble Wars for children aged five to eleven, or working with footwork, pivoting to zero, or in opposition to the dummy player, and then using one foot off on the foot that pivots. Through the exercises, you're training your technique and accuracy as well as playing games where they are putting these techniques into practice with a sense of fun that helps you learn faster and mimics the random nature of the sport the students are learning. In addition, we suggest including shooting drills as well as playing games one-on-one during every session as shooting is considered among the most important abilities in basketball. One at a time is a good technique to develop fundamentals for defensive and offensive as well as getting the ball into more hands of players simultaneously. The final chapter this book is the complete list of drills as well as games suited to certain different ages, which could be used as a guide when making plans and adding diversity to your schedule during the course of the season.

While putting your plan of practice in place, Bob Hurley Sr. is one of the most effective high school coaches to ever be found in the United States, recommends a two-third practice of skill-building to a one-third of team playing. In an hour-long practice, for children aged 9 and over around twenty minutes could be dedicated to four-on-four or five on five or four in five group play, if is appropriate. Additionally, skill work does not be limited to the one-on-one drills for skill development however it should be a mix of competitive breakdown drills and games. Also, he advised sticking to the written plan of practice to the best of your ability and, if you find that the idea doesn't work for you over longer periods of time, and revisit it on the following day, and we believe. A drill segment should not typically be longer than 10 minutes, with a minimum of waiting in the line.

Regarding the length of practice and duration, we suggest 45 to 60 minutes to two times each week for children ages five up to eighteen years old. 45 to 75 minutes twice times per week, for children 9-12 years old and sixty-nine to ninety minutes twice to every week for children between the ages of twelve and fourteen 14 years older. Also, John Wooden, in his book They Call Me Coach says, "End practice on a happy note." It is possible by doing the drill your team is most fond of or playing a sport. This is why we are not recommending exercising following the practice.

The Parent Meeting

Parents exert a huge influence over their children, so it's important to be involved with their influence to ensure the positive environment. It is recommended to adopt an inclusive attitude instead of one that is confrontational because parents who are clear and supportive generally have coachable excuse that help their children. At your next parent-teacher meeting, an ideal agenda could be to give a quick overview of you (no requirement to mention the achievements or awards you've received) as well as your team's fundamental principles and values, and clear expectations regarding the coach-parent relationship, play timing considerations, logistical and timing, and then conclude by addressing any concerns.

By having distinct core values, you create a positive foundation for behaviour regardless of whether you are on the court. Also, it becomes apparent to parents that you are concerned about more than basketball and that you are concerned about the development of your child's character as a whole. Parents will also gain an comprehension of the things that guide your choices and aid in promoting. We don't recommend an extensive list of rules that go beyond the core values, but instead the two or four rules for your children that you and your parents are aware of. A good example of a standard could include having fun, putting in a great efforts, staying punctual, and not complain or whining.

Discussion of the relationship between coach and player helps establish clear expectations for communication. Concerning the parent-coach relationship, parents should be aware of your coaching principles and values as well as the requirements for team members and scheduling along with fees and your playing times are determined. We as coaches expect parents to voice their concerns directly to us rather than directly in front of their children in response to their influence. The issue should not be discussed right after the event, since in times of emotional turmoil, the right words or decisions should not be made. Parents should help their children to express any issues they might need to discuss with their coach by enlisting the support of their parents and inform you about any scheduled conflicts ahead of time if they are appropriate. The things that you can ask parents to discuss with their as a coach would be the way they treat their child physical or mental or behavioral issues that their child may be experiencing, as well as strategies to assist your child to improve. However, we do not advise against team-based strategies, game calls, or discussions with the other players on your team not to be discussed. Also, we recommend that you do not discuss the timing of games if it's at your coach's decision at the time that you coach. This is something will be discussed later on in this section.

The parent-player relationship is a good example. Bruce Brown, founder of Proactive Coaching, recommends that whenever your child is within a secure and safe environment, "Release your child to the game." When acting as a parent you can increase your child's involvement as well as their enjoyment and desire to play basketball. As parents, raising the bar to our children with regard to their effort and morals can be acceptable provided it's under their control (not dependent on the outcome) and is clearly communicated. Additionally, parents must stay away from the PGA as well as post-game evaluation, because if they do it consistently it can be harmful to children's enjoyment sport.

To build a relationship between coach and player inform your players that they are welcome for discussion about playing times and also to address any issues you be having in a professional and straightforward way. Explain to them that it takes bravery, which you admire. It is also advisable to tell your players not to compare their own performance to other players and instead focus on things they are able to manage, like their attitude and efforts. As a coach it's crucial that you establish your expectations and requirements for your players are clear and crystal clear.

The issue of playing time can increase because players grow older and the playing time becomes equally. To be in line with USA Youth Basketball we recommend equal time to play for players aged seven to eight years of age, equal playing time for players aged 9-11 years old and coaches' discretion during the final 2 to 4 minute of each game as well as full discretion of coaches for players aged 12+ and utilizing common sense. So long as there's no issues of serious conduct, it is recommended that all of your children participates the game and participates. The majority of youth organizations offer clear guidelines you must follow regarding playing time and may be slightly different from the above guidelines, such as equal time for playing through sixth grade, with the discretion of coaches adhering to. As a youth teacher, these rules can be shared with your parents. In the event that it's a decision of the coach, for the age group you're coaching, there could be a myriad of aspects that affect the decision of you or your team regarding the time your child plays. These elements should be made clear to the parents of your players and their children as well as their skill level as well as behavior and commitment to work, athleticism as well as game and practice performances, as well as possible match-up considerations.

Chapter 3: Skill Development

Some research shows that the "Golden Age of Skill Development" can be found between the ages of eight and twelve years old, due to the development of brain cells occurring rapidly as well as the body's ability to be enough advanced with its physical growth. This time frame to develop and acquire skills is believed to be the ideal stage for kids to learn and build their sports abilities. However, this doesn't mean the skills can't be improved later however, they may require longer in later years. This does not mean that children should be specialized in one sport as young as they are. There's a lot of evidence to suggest that the focus of a particular sport in this early age can be harmful to the long-term growth of a child. It is crucial to understand is that team strategies and teamwork should not have the precedence over development of skills in practicing and the coach of youth ought to be an expert in developing skills. If your athletes have bad shots or are unable to dribble using their hands even when they're fifteen year old and are in High School, then the likelihood that they will put in an enormous amount of effort to build and enhance their skills in order to improve is low.

If your players can't shoot or pass, dribble or pivot, it will no matter which offensive plan or plan you come up with. The quality of players and the culture they represent will always outweigh strategies and play. Many examples show this, and an instance is The Golden State Warriors of 2019-2020. The Warriors had a great record in the time prior to that, having multiple All-Star players on their roster and numerous championships however due to the injuries sustained by Steph Curry as well as Klay Thompson and Kevin Durant leaving the team the Warriors became an below average team. They had the same excellent coaching staff and strategy, however the players were different. This is the reason why effective coaching in the early years to help players develop is crucial and the reason why coaching for youth is crucial. One reason Iceland with an estimated population of 325,000 is home to seventy of the top professional soccer players from Europe is due to the fact that from the age of a child, they learn from experienced licensed coaches.

In the field of education, there are standard test of proficiency in Math as well as Reading and also for training in strength. the testing of baselines is conducted in order for later to collect comparison measures and evaluate the efficacy of teaching or training. But, when it comes to basketball, young coaches don't take the time to gather the baseline measures of their skills, such as the basketball report card or even have clear expectations about what they should achieve for certain age groups. When you conduct the report card for the development of skills, you're informing your children and parents that this developing matter is vital and you, as coach, are concerned about the development of your players in this field. Peter Drucker, the legendary consultant in management, stated that the things that are measured improve. This training and testing process into three phases of age: from five to 8 years of age, 9 to twelve years old and 12-14 years old.

Now we'll be technical and geek out regarding the growth of our skills over the next couple of paragraphs, so take your time. From ages 5 to 8 years old, there are six fundamental skills that we're trying to develop including getting into the triple threat position jumping stop and pivoting properly stationary dribbling techniques both hands on the left and right, running while dribbling the ball using right and left hand with the head raised, basic shooting techniques that are not focused on the rim, and a correct technique of passing for chest and bounce passes. On our Members page at youthbasketballdevelopment.com there are age specific drills and games with bullet point teaching techniques to address all six of these skills. To test your skills in a standardized manner for the stage at which they are developing, there are four types of tests. These are. Demonstration of jumping stopping to a triple threat and pivot before throwing the correct pass with no travel with a coach or parent. 2. Do ten pounds of dribbling with left hand, ten pounds Dribbles using the left hand and ten crosses in 14 seconds or less while the head raised. 3. Jog at a jog speed using both hands, twenty feet below and return to the start by putting your head upwards. 4. Show proper form of shooting by shooting the ball not in the rim, but up into the air, before the coach or parent. The book includes a sample testing worksheet for each of the three phases of development within the library section near the bottom of the book as well as take home drilling sheets. From ages 8-12 years of age, also known as"the "Golden Age of Skill Acquisition" There are four major skill areas that we're focusing on, which include feetwork and pivoting, to include direct drive as well as the crossover step; ball handling, which includes complete speed dribbling using the left and right hand and a change in speed as well as one direction change move, shooting basics from the rim and with the proper height and the first stages of finishing in the edge. There are video examples of all of these skill areas and testing at youthbasketballdevelopment.com as well as drills and games to address on the Members page. There are only four tests that test these abilities. They comprise: 1. Demonstration of the v-series drill (cross-overs between legs using the right foot in front, and between legs while putting left foot forward 15 times per) within twenty minutes or less, with the head raised. 2. Perform a full speed lay-up by alternating left and right hands for a parent or a coach on one foot. 3. Show proper form using straight driving, cross-over steps, shot fakes, and create an open space off the left foot to show right-handed players. Players should be able to communicate with a teacher or parent playing at a high speed. 4. Practice a proper shot by pointing a ball towards the rim and the coach or parent from a suitable range.

In our 3rd phase of development in skill for children 12-14 years, we have four areas that we would like to improve and focus on that include ball handling in a symmetrical manner both hands, beginning to master the one or two moves of a dribble properly executing movement and pivoting using jabs and the ability to align to the edge at different angles as well as the progression of final moves towards the rim, as well as the grooving, and repeating of correct shooting technique off of the dribble catch. Again, video examples can be found at youthbasketballdevelopment.com with drills and games to address on the Members page. Five tests that can be used to establish an initial measure of effectiveness and establish the quality of instruction are: 1. Demonstration and demonstration of the pound series (pound cross-over or pound between legs or in the rear) 1 minute timed of sixty times or more. 2. Show ninety percent or more hand symmetry in a the speed dribble test while head-up. 3. Perform a full-speed lay-up reverse using the left and right hands using correct form and technique to your coach or parent. 4. Show proper form using the jab-series footwork from left foot of left handed players in front of parents or coaches in game-speed. 5. Develop the ability to square with the inside foot, and then shoot the ball in a proper manner using self-pass. In the chapter on practice planning, We believe that the most effective method of teaching and developing this skill is to train the technique and then play the skill.

The students we train can't only have to be "drill guys or girls". It is the case with a student who is very attractive in drills, however when it comes to playing they struggle to create plays. There must be an equilibrium of "drilling" (technique training) and engaging in a game (one at one two-on-two and five on five and so on...). That's why we suggest playing in a situation this skill that we have were just drilling. An example would be after our pivoting/footwork/finishing skill work your team would play one on one off the pivot foot with three to four dribbles maximum for the offense. In the end, by ending the skill section with a drill that is similar to a game, it ends the exercise in a positive way and speed up the process of learning.

The way we have divided the development of skills into the ball handling, pivoting/footwork getting to the rim, shooting, and pass areas by incorporating offensive team concepts defense concepts for teams, as well as particular situations covered in our section on strategy. It is generally said that the simplicity of teaching and the enthusiasm is the most important thing to teach. The more you speak, your students off, the more chance you have of losing the students, so we suggest 3-4 bullet points for teaching an ability that will instantly alert players to the right direction. Bullet point instruction was borrowed from the legendary Kevin Eastman, a former college and NBA coach. If you're able to show the ability for your students, more effective. If you don't have the highest level of skill If you observe the players in your group demonstrating the skill or drill in correctly, have them show it to the class and tell them what we'd like to see it look like. For instance, when teaching two foot finishes near the rim, our bullet points for instruction would be eyes upwards towards the rim ball towards the outside shoulder (don't get pregnant by the ball) as well as a low, solid base. Bullet points like these help to provide a clear understanding of the ability and guide the point across in a quick, short and easy manner. If you say don't get too tense with the ball, the player is aware of how to bring it on the outside shoulder to shield it from being snatched by defenders. It also gives more room between the ball and opponent. The drills as well as games listed on the Members' page include specific bullet points for instructors in understanding which points to focus on. Another option to develop an image of words to make your athletes low and athletic in the event of a ball is to tell them that they are an ostrich, not a cheetah. Cheetahs have a low, quick speed and giraffes stand taller and less athletic. You can be a cheetah if you are playing ball, not the Giraffe.

It has also been observed that players who can handle balls well tend to be excellent passers because they are able to move their dribbles and pivot while keeping their eyes upwards. They are better able to see and, as a result, are able to discern open teammates as well as better detect movement on the field. So, that it's crucial in the early years of youth that you send out 5 to 10 minutes ball handling sheets to the players to perform between practice sessions generally twice a week at the earliest age.

Home drill sheets are a rapid, concentrated and planned practice instruction in technique and offer the player with a better foundation that will allow for more creativity in playing situations. Start with two or one balls stationary exercises. The younger the child, the longer they have to dedicate to these drills and constantly focusing on developing the capacity to hit and to become a ball speed. If they're able to do the drill 10 times in the same row, allow them to begin taking thirty-second timings. What is the fastest speed they can cross the ball or move it in their thighs? The stationary drills are a good option, and can be practiced at home, are essential to build a foundation that will allow them to get playing basketball. To motivate them to continue practicing these at-home drills, it is recommended to give your athletes some small rewards like stickers on their water bottles or small drinks for sports at the end of two or four weeks of constant execution. It's important to make sure your players know that the better they get, the more enjoyable the game will be as it turns into "Showtime" on the court where everyone is able to pass, shoot and dribble with ease. For players who have a disadvantage, make sure they don't think about how they compare to other players and remember that regardless of the place they're at but the direction they're headed to which is the most important thing. If you can have your players take part in a one-on-one game at home, following drilling sheet's conclusion, more effective.

Strategy

There are numerous efficient ways to enjoy the basketball game. On offense, you could run an offensive motion or a continuity offense several set plays, or even a mix of those mentioned. In defense, you may be man-to-man, and press the passing lanes, or you can be within the gap, in the in the zone and pressure all the different methods. The engine behind these methods is strong players. If you're managing a team of youth, there usually the local high school or an association that you're a member of. This will to guide you in the strategy you'll teach. It is so that things don't change from year to year, resulting in greater proficiency and ensures that there's a consistent communication system that contributes to better comprehension. If you're responsible for choosing your team's offensive or defensive plan, we believe that the phrase "jack of all trades master of none" is applicable. We believe that, at the earliest age level, when you're teaching various defensive and offensive techniques or more than two or three different plays, you're detracting too much from the development of your players during your training sessions. You focus too much in the short term on success rather than longer-term growth. Also, if you keep the process straightforward, it will lead to greater spontaneity and faster choices which allow to run more efficiently practices that focus on the focus on skill development and not strategy concentration. The initial strategy we'll discuss is offensive team's concepts.

In the early years, We believe in a progressive motion offensive approach throughout the 9-14 stage and believe that only a small amount of pre-planned strategies should be used. Particularly the motion offense (examples include a five-out motion, dribble drive reading and reacting motion and a four out one which allows for the player to be interchangeable) permits players to take on a variety of roles. This is a great way of teaching in a progressively manner with cutting and spacing initially being taught and moving to screen actions when necessary. It is crucial that your coaches at the high school level or association leaders be included with the offensive team system that is best used.

The principal reasons to teach motion offense as well as having a few sets plays is that It prepares players for the offensive systems could be involved towards the end of their growth, enables players to become more intuitive and helps develop decision-making as well as a more enjoyable way of playing and provides opportunities for all players to play or contribute every possession a game. While teaching offensive motion concepts, it is also a time to work on developing skills while also learning a specific set play sequence. All of this leads to increased effectiveness of team practices.

Establishing the foundations of team offensive ideas earlier in the youth development program helps improve the mastery of ability to execute, and a greater level of confidence when they reach a later stage. If your goal was to conduct set play at a young age, you could be successful for a short time, however later on, decisions and development will be impeded. In addition, if everyone in the age range of the youth group use the same offensive terms and progressing this can improve understanding and cohesion when players progress.

Set plays, also known as continuity offenses are a crucial element for offensive basketball. But, it is not uncommon to listen to coaches yelling at players to execute the ball, but then the player will not pay attention to the open shot, lane or a teammate. In some cases, an offense that is more fluid could result in bad offensive plays, however generally being able to create plays with a structure can be used quite efficiently (this is when the level of skill is really helpful). It is essential for players to stay that they are on the field and playing the game rather than conduct the play. In order to improve the ability of your players, increase their awareness of the possibilities and not limit the attention on a single entry in the set game.

We believe that players are more comfortable when they can create plays and also have choices to choose from instead of running an undefined play every game to your two or one top players. In these situations, only a couple of players hold the ball at their fingertips all the time and improve, but it is difficult to judge the performance of the other players in the court. A motion offense is a game where everyone should be aware of the best shot for them, and may get a chance to score or play the play every time they step on the court. This goes along with the concept of having fun while improving the level of skill.

In the past, we have discussed some basic and effective offensive strategies for young basketball players include a five-out motion or dribble drive reading and reacting motion and a four out one-in-motion and the player "in" being interchangeable. Our Members' page offer a progression of teaching that includes diagrams of the five-out motion offense, with cutting as well as dribble penetration initially followed by screening exercises in later stages of growth.

Chapter 4: Motion Cutting Teaching Progression

1. Pivoting/Footwork - One on Zero instruction of direct drive crossing-over step, lifting false, and then rip the pivots to make feet in space. Do one game on the one foot off of pivot (three to four dribbles maximum).

2. V-Cut and L Cut A single V-Cut and L-Cut training using footwork. Try one game on V-Cut as well as L-Cut (three to four dribbles maximum).

3. Three-on-zero Motion Cutting teaching spacing, and including V-Cuts, L-Cuts, as well as Addition Of Give and Go as well as Back Cuts. Cut the floor hard, and then stretch the floor by cutting the exit.

4. Three on Three on Motion Cutting: The emphasis is on spacing and squarering all the way to the the rim. You can incorporate restrictions on dribbles, as

well as the number of passes prior to scoring.

5. Five Zero Motion Cutting Walking through space/positioning on the floor. Include V-Cuts, L Cuts, Back Cuts and Giving and Going Cuts. Add post-ups for a second counting. Be patient!

6. Five Zero Motion Entries Limit this to not more than two or three entries. For example, entries on the down screen and dribbles at an entry cut back, ball screens or floppy crossing-screen entry.

7. Five on Five on Half Court: Focus is on spacing, and entering the paint from the dribble, passing and cut actions, or an after finish.

8. Five on Zero, and Five Five Transition: May be assigned a point guard, or fillers or pushers based on your level of skill and preferences. The pushers could lift the ball

off the to the floor while fillers can fill in lanes.

Defensive Strategy

Then we will go straight to the main point. for children ages 12 and under, the zone defense must be used as a man against player or man-to defensive game. This helps develop the personal skills involved in protecting a player off the ball and. When playing zone defense at these early ages, coaches have chosen to place emphasis on the winning of a game or tournament instead of long-term improvement. A majority of the players aged between eight and 12 years young struggle to deal with the shooting in the perimeter from the three-point line as well as throwing skip passes watching defenders go off, and then throwing the ball in the opposite way and also having a comfortable ball being in the middle of the area. This is what can make a zone defense efficient for young players. Do your best to resist any temptation you need to exploit these inherent flaws at this age to either make a difference in the outcome of a game, or to ensure your team is in the match. Actually, FIBA (International Basketball Federation) enforces an "no zone defense" rule that applies to players who are under 14 years old and the intention is to aid in the growth of the young athletes in both defensive and offensive ways.

We recommend you introduce a player to players or a man to man defense in the ages of 14 and younger. Our library section provide a comprehensive teaching curriculum that includes games and drills specifically designed for each stage of growth. The games and drills address the fundamental defense concepts like correct stance, vision communication, anticipation, and unity. As you create your defensive plan to understand how you'll protect the posts (play behind a three-quarter denial, or fully dead front) be able to keep one pass clear of the ball (be in the gap, or denial) and also guard balls screens (help to recover the ball, catch and recover, trap or switch) to ensure clarity and effectiveness. Jack Bennett, former head coach at the university of Wisconsin-StevensPoint and two-time NCAA Division III National Champion stated that if you're team is athletically superior to the majority of teams you take on, you should be able to get out and block one pass away. Or, you can play it in the gaps.

It is recommended that you play at a time during each practice to be you can improve your ball defense as well as incorporate the defense in transition into the practice program. If your team is struggling to guard the ball, or is unable to create an offense that is against a specific defense, it will be difficult to defend anyone. The importance of rebounding is emphasized by completing each practice by rebounding throughout the exercise. Finally, defensive break-down exercises (one on one or two on two three on three and four-on-four) are strongly recommended as they require the defense to need to fill more spaces.

Situations

When you team moves closer for playing in competitive matches, it's crucial to incorporate some easy base out of bounds (BLOBs) as well as sideline out of bounds (SLOB) and press breakers that are incorporated. Remember to keep the actions easy and you are free to adapt these to the strengths of your team. At times, it is helpful to have a 10 to fifteen minutes period of your training, specifically for players aged 9-14 in order to review scenarios that could arise in the game, such as the free throw situation, fully courted, the jumping ball scenario, trying to attack an area defense when your tournament in permits this or even playing one minute ending of the game can be a fun way to plan and create clear plans. The examples of all these scenarios and actions are available within the section on library.

Game Coaching

Don't be the young coach who is working with as an official. Coaches set the standard for your children and their parents throughout the game. If you're complaining about the movement of screens, travels or fouls that aren't being reported, then your parents are likely to have to be complaining from the stands too and your players ' body communication and mental toughness will be affected. Basketball officials for youth aren't professional and they will make a few mistakes. It's normal. be human and try the best you can not say something negative or become officiating from the sidelines. It will allow you to stay concentrated in your present and better coach your team.

Long-Term Development

Research has revealed that a focus on performance and the short-term results (pseudo youth state championships, wins rankings, and winning) in sports for youth could hinder the advantages of participating and increase the likelihood of burnout, injuries, and detachment from physical activities. Also, the emphasis on results that are short-term at the juvenile level can cause early single sport specificization as well as intense training in the early years of childhood. The state tournaments and rankings have a focus on results and based on winning. In this way, state tournaments and rankings naturally place outcomes and winning before growth and participation. The research also suggests that the competitive performance at stage of youth is not as significant, in the best case, or perhaps very little to the achievement at the high school level.

Physically mature teams in the youth level tend to be successful. As a child, we couldn't beat our two league rivals, Northwestern and Barron, in middle school (fourteen and less). They were larger than us and larger. In high school, we played on the team that took home multiple league championships and made it to the state championship twice. Two teams on the other side were physically more advanced than we, however the difference in their physical abilities was not as significant in the later years as our ability as well as our passion for football was growing, leading to greater success later on down the line.

The other end of the coin, if you coach a young team who is achieving success with a high percentage of success, be sure to remind parents and players that losses and wins at a young age don't mean anything more than building our positive core values, relationships as well as improving and having a blast. This kind of mindset is results-oriented rather than process orientated, and at the youth stage has been proven that it can lead to lasting achievement. Associations and parents that concentrate on making small changes and developing an attitude of work versus outcomes and wins tend to have an inclination to be competitive and growth-oriented and highly-performers.

For a warning, we have seen a 6th grader walking in the Summer community parade carrying the banner that stated they taken home the "Sixth Grade State Championship". It did not state that all schools of similar size as well as associations across the state took part. Most of the situations, that is not the situation. To participate, an enormous entry cost could be required, which may deter people with lower incomes from taking part. School and parent groups may opt not to participate due to transportation, conflicting dates and cost concerns. Sometimes, teams be required to take part in several previous tournaments run by the company that runs"the "State Tournament". The sixth grade team was unable to beat more than two consecutive games during the playoffs at high school. It also had several issues with parents relating to pressure and unrealistic expectations to succeed.

Chapter 5: Progressive Teaching Plan

The progressive plan of instruction offers a long-term roadmap to ensure individual and team performance. The plan allows players to participate and analyze the game by them, instead of relying on multiple sets of practices and routines. In addition, by having basic skill measurements and having an understanding of the things that is expected at certain levels of development, your decisions that you make as a coach is better and the practices are much more specific and effective. Between five and fourteen years old, we've broken down our curriculum of progressive instruction into three distinct phases that are phase I, the beginning Phase (five to eighteen years old) and phase II the Basic Principles Phase (eight to twelve years old) as well as phase III, the Developed Phase (twelve to 14 one year old). The previous mention was in our chapter on skill development and in our skill development chapter.

The Beginning Phase (five up to 8 years old) In the Beginning Phase, emphasis is on having fun as well as the basics of capabilities. Six fundamental skills which we hope to achieve were mentioned in the chapter on skill development. Our Members' page offer all the skill and strategy subjects covered with the appropriate exercises and games. It is not recommended to play five on five in this stage or to spend any long time playing five-on-5 offensive and defensive techniques. The rim heights and the ball dimensions should be right for better performance. The suggested levels of rim and ball are also available inside our Library section. It includes easy five- to 10-minute drill sheets that you can take home.

In the basic principles Phase (eight to twelve years young) also known as"the "Golden Age", skill advancement is accelerated to an appropriate shooting posture around the rim. This includes crossing-over steps and direct drive footwork. It also teaches change of direction, change of speed in relation to ball handling and other techniques to end with the center. It's a crucial moment to establish a strong base for technique for shooting and handling the ball by the hand. The progression from strategy to five on five defensive as well as offensive strategies is executed in this stage and focuses on spacing, cutting and dribble strategies.

In the final stage which is called it is the Developed Phase (twelve through 14 year teenagers) The teaching will hopefully be moved to ball handling using identical symmetry between both hands. In addition, starting with mastery of just one or two dribble movements, squareing upwards at the rim with various angles, the progression of finishing steps on the rim, as well as practicing grooving as well as a repetition of the correct shot form after the dribble and catch is further developed. If seventy-eight percent of kids on your team will be able to start their high school age (fifteen years or more) having the capability to dribble and reach the rim with both hand, shoot in proper shot form (great follow-through, only just one shot, and a solid base) and pivot under pressure. If you've achieved a phenomenal job in improving the skills of the team. But more important is when your team is filled with passion for sports and has a strong work ethic and is able to listen to others, it is a huge plus for the human race. Games and drills that are that are associated with the development of skills and the strategy to achieve this are available within our Library section.

How long should your child's basketball schedule be? The most time during the year of organized basketball is recommended to be four months for kids ages eight and younger, five to six months for those between nine and eleven seven months for those between 12 and 14 and fourteen years old. If your players go over these limits, there is a higher chance of injury as well as burnout, breakdown, and injury.

Fun

Fun is the final research issue. As per Professor. Amanda Visek in her journal article entitled "Toward Understanding Youth Athletes' Fun Priorities: An Investigation of Sex, Age, and Levels of Play", "What counts most for both boys and girls is aspects like putting your best effort into at work, being physically active, and performing well with a partner. The findings are similar in athletes of young and old ages, and between competitive and recreational different levels of competition." As a junior coach it's essential to recognize these enjoyable aspects and make them a priority. The greater fun your team's experiencing, the more they'll be engaged in sports, and will be able to have positive effects over the long down the road.

Chapter 6: The Rules Of Basketball

However, if you're coaching younger players, these rules can be easily forgotten once they take the floor.

The three-second rule (which we'll discuss later in this article) is just one of many great examples.

But before you can teach the rules to your team, you must know them yourself.

So keep reading, because by the end of this article, you'll be up to speed on all the basketball rules so you can teach your players and help them develop throughout the season!

The Rules

Basketball is a team sport.

Two teams of five players each try to score by shooting a ball through a hoop elevated 10 feet above the ground.

The game is played on a rectangular floor called the court, and there is a hoop at each end.

The court is divided into two main sections by the mid-court line.

If the offensive team puts the ball into play behind the mid-court line, it has ten seconds to get the ball over the mid-court line.

If it doesn't, then the defense gets the ball.

Once the offensive team gets the ball over the mid-court line, it can no longer have possession of the ball in the area behind the midcourt line.

If it does, the defense is awarded the ball.

Basketball Court 1

The ball is moved down the court toward the basket by passing or dribbling. The team with the ball is called the offense.

The team without the ball is called the defense.

The defense tries to steal the ball, contest shots, deflect passes, and garner rebounds.

Points

When a team makes a basket, they score two points and the ball goes to the other team.

If a basket, or field goal, is made outside of the three-point arc, then that basket is worth three points. A free throw is worth one point.

Free throws are awarded to a team according to some formats involving the number of fouls committed in a half and/or the type of foul committed.

Fouling a shooter always results in two or three free throws being awarded the shooter, depending upon where he was when he shot. If he was beyond the three-point line, then he gets three shots.

Other types of fouls do not result in free throws being awarded until a certain number have accumulated during a half (called "team fouls").

Once that number is reached, then the player who was fouled is awarded a '1-and-1' opportunity. If he makes his first free throw, he gets to attempt a second. If he misses the first shot, the ball is live on the rebound.

Game Clock

Each game is divided into sections, and all levels have two halves.

In college, each half is twenty minutes long.

In high school and below, the halves are divided into eight (and sometimes, six) minute quarters. In the pros, quarters are twelve minutes long.

There is a gap of several minutes between halves. Gaps between quarters are relatively short.

If the score is tied at the end of regulation, then overtime periods of various lengths are played until a winner emerges.

Basket Assignment and Tip-Off

Also, each team is assigned a basket or goal to defend.

This means that the other basket is their scoring basket.

At halftime, the teams switch goals.

The game begins with one player from either team at center court.

A referee will toss the ball up between the two. The player that gets his hands on the ball will tip it to a teammate. This is called a tip-off.

Fouls and Violations

In addition to stealing the ball from an opposing player, there are other ways for a team to get the ball.

One such way is if the other team commits a foul or violation.

FOULS

Recommended Resources for Youth Coaches

Coaching Youth Basketball Successfully

60+ Youth Basketball Drills

Simple Offense for Youth Basketball

Personal fouls: Personal fouls include any type of illegal physical contact.

Hitting

Pushing

Slapping

Holding

Illegal pick/screen -- when an offensive player is moving. When an offensive player sticks out a limb and makes physical contact with a defender in an attempt to block the path of the defender.

Personal foul penalties: If a player is shooting while a being fouled, then he gets two free throws if his shot doesn't go in, but only one free throw if his shot does go in.

Three free throws are awarded if the player is fouled while shooting for a three-point goal and they miss their shot. If a player is fouled while shooting a three-point shot and makes it anyway, he is awarded one free throw. Thus, he could score four points on the play.

Inbounds. If fouled while not shooting, the ball is given to the team the foul was committed upon. They get the ball at the nearest side or baseline, out of bounds, and have 5 seconds to pass the ball onto the court.

One & one. If the team committing the foul has seven or more fouls in the game, then the player who was fouled is awarded one free throw. If he makes his first shot, then he is awarded another free throw.

Ten or more fouls. If the team committing the foul has ten or more fouls, then the fouled player receives two free throws.

Charging. An offensive foul that is committed when a player pushes or runs over a defensive player. The ball is given to the team that the foul was committed upon.

Blocking. Blocking is illegal personal contact resulting from a defender not establishing position in time to prevent an opponent's drive to the basket.

Flagrant foul. Violent contact with an opponent. This includes hitting, kicking, and punching. This type of foul results in free throws plus the offense retaining possession of the ball after the free throws.

Intentional foul. When a player makes physical contact with another player with no reasonable effort to steal the ball. It is a judgment call for the officials.

Technical foul. Technical foul. A player or a coach can commit this type of foul. It does not involve player contact or the ball but is instead about the 'manners' of the game. Foul language, obscenity, obscene gestures, and even arguing can be considered a technical foul, as can technical details regarding filling in the scorebook improperly or dunking during warm-ups.

VIOLATIONS

Walking/Traveling. Taking more than 'a step and a half' without dribbling the ball is traveling. Moving your pivot foot once you've stopped dribbling is traveling.

Carrying/palming. When a player dribbles the ball with his hand too far to the side of or, sometimes, even under the ball.

Double Dribble. Dribbling the ball with both hands on the ball at the same time or picking up the dribble and then dribbling again is a double dribble.

Held ball. Occasionally, two or more opposing players will gain possession of the ball at the same time. In order to avoid a prolonged and/or violent tussle, the referee stops the action and awards the ball to one team or the other on a rotating basis.

Goaltending. If a defensive player interferes with a shot while it's on the way down toward the basket, while it's on the way up toward the basket after having touched the backboard, or while it's in the cylinder above the rim, it's goaltending and the shot counts. If committed by an offensive player, it's a violation and the ball is awarded to the opposing team for a throw-in.

Backcourt violation. Once the offense has brought the ball across the mid-court line, they cannot go back across the line during possession. If they do, the ball is awarded to the other team to pass inbounds.

Time restrictions. A player passing the ball inbounds has five seconds to pass the ball. If he does not, then the ball is awarded to the other team. Other time restrictions include the rule that a player cannot have the ball for more than five seconds when being closely guarded and, in some states and levels, shot-clock restrictions requiring a team to attempt a shot within a given time frame.

Player Positions

Center. Centers are generally your tallest players. They generally are positioned near the basket.

Offensive -- The center's goal is to get open for a pass and to shoot. They are also responsible for blocking defenders, known as picking or screening, to open other players up for driving to the basket for a goal. Centers are expected to get some offensive rebounds and put-backs.

Defensive -- On defense, the center's main responsibility is to keep opponents from shooting by blocking shots and passes in the key area. They also are expected to get a lot of rebounds because they're taller.

Forward. Your next tallest players will most likely be your forwards. While a forward may be called upon to play under the hoop, they may also be required to operate in the wings and corner areas.

Offensive -- Forwards are responsible to get free for a pass, take outside shots, drive for goals, and rebound.

Defensive -- Responsibilities include preventing drives to the goal and rebounding.

Guard. These are potentially your shortest players and they should be really good at dribbling fast, seeing the court, and passing. It is their job to bring the ball down the court and set up offensive plays.

Chapter 7: Basketball For Beginners

As an amateur, starting out might be very difficult for you if you don't know the fundamentals of the game. It is, therefore, mandatory that you begin with the basic things like dribbling, passing and shooting. Basketball has a small number of drills designed to help you as a total beginner to easily learn the offensive and defensive principles.

Knowing these drills will accelerate your learning curve for the hoops. And this will eventually help you easily advance and perfect your overall basketball skills in a shorter period of time. Below are the 4 main skills you need to know as a trainee;

#1. Ball handling

The first skill is how you handle the ball. Basketball mainly entails dribbling the ball around the court. Therefore, you need to learn some dripping movements so that you familiarize with the ball handling.

Doing some dribble tags, stationary drills and tight chairs enables you to appropriately move the ball during your training session.

Dribble tags- this one is done with other trainees. As you dribble the ball, all other players need to avoid being tagged by someone having the ball. You need to be constant in dribbling.

Stationary drills- here you attempt some drooling in a circular motion around your legs at varied heights. You can also train by dribbling the ball through your legs without moving around the court.

Tight chairs-this skill is usually done with six chairs. You need to arrange them in two rows of three chairs each. Now you have to dribble around each chair with different skills like figure 8

#2. Shooting

For you to be able to score points in this port you need to know how to shoot. All beginners need to learn this skill and the various techniques of shooting.

We have the box drill and the air-ball drill.

Shooting basketball

In the air-ball drill, there must be several players each with a ball. You all get in an offensive position, dropping your elbows, jumping and shooting from your highest points.

Box drill is carried out with one ball but with players on the right and left side on the court. Player on the right takes a jump shot to the backyard while the left side players run up to receive the rebound making their own shot. The ball then moves from one player to another on the right side for drill continuousness.

#3. Passing

This is the most critical part. You need to get the ball to your co-players.

Being a learner, you need to know how to make decent passes throughout the game. You need to practice some chest passes with other trainees. Also, overhead passes are allowed in this sport thus learning how to go about them is key. You need to keep the ball directly above your head.

Bounce passes are also important in basketball. Here as you pass the ball, you target the floor about three-quarters between you and your teammate.

#4. Offensive /Defensive drills

It is required that you learn to be either an offender or a defender. During this game, there will be a lot of game shifts going on hence you must train the offensive/defensive drills.

An Offensive drill: This is a struggle with players divided and lined up under each basket. First players from both sides dribble at full speed to the opposite baskets as the next players are all set to grip the rebound and repeat the drill.

A defensive drill: As you practice this, you need two players standing in between from the ball. One defensive and the other offensive. After the signal, the defensive player uses his/her position to keep the other player from getting the ball.

Where to play basketball

Basketball court dimension

The sport can take place indoors or outdoors. This all depends on your comfortability and where you prefer best.

This game is played on a basketball court. Avail yourself at any nearest court where you can be able to practice. If you don't have any around your neighborhood don't worry. This sport can also be played in the gym because they have an area set aside for practicing basic skills.

However, as a learner, you should not play at public courts because you might feel challenged by the experts hence give up. Some of the places best for playing are;

Backyard

Gym

Schoolyards or playgrounds

Community center facilities

Mounting hoops on the garage

Take your game to the next level

Do you wish to be like the professionals in basketball?

Getting yourself a good coach will be of great help here. You should find one who has built experience with the game and good at training for you to become skilled.

You need to know the shooting. You will only score points through shooting in this sport. It is for this reason you need to learn how to become an effective shooter. Additionally, you must learn how to be able to stop a catch from an opponent.

Dribbling as you move around the court is also very technical. It is very necessary for you to learn on how to dribble without losing balance. This can only be achieved through knowing the right posture. Knowledge of how to place your feet and arms is significant.

Jumping in this game is important too. High jumps will allow you to collect rebounds, shooting and blocking shots from your opponents. Therefore, you must learn how to correctly jump in the game.

There are some secrets that will help you focus on your objective. A good warm-up will help you raise your heart rate before you start your training.

Tips:

You should always dribble the ball with your weak hand. This will enable you to handle the ball with both hands.

Never give up. If you feel like you have taken too long to be perfect you should never give up. Persistence is the key to excellence.

As a beginner, always ask tips from your trainer or other skilled players. By doing this, you will be able to learn the game faster.

Drink enough water. This game involves a lot of running. Running leads to sweating thus water loss from the body. You need to take enough water to prevent dehydration.

If you think you want to avoid ankel injury, you need a pair of shoes for ankle support, get it! Also, you can get ankle brace too!

Buy basketball socks that prevent blisters.

Having proper basketball shorts will help too!

Warning:

Get some rest. This activity can be very tiresome thus if you feel worn out, stop and take some rest. This being a fun game, you should not make the process strenuous for your body.

You also need to be keen on whichever step you are taking. Concentrate on the drills so that you are able to learn faster and master the game.

Baller's Guide

A Beginner's Guide to Getting Started in Basketball

Step #1: Get into the Correct Gear

Before you jump into a pickup game or have your kiddo attend their first practice, it is important for the right basketball gear to be available. The right gear will support your game. The wrong gear could lead to an embarrassing situation, an injury, or other problematic issues.

Here are the key elements to gear that you'll want to consider.

Step #1. Shoes.

Good basketball shoes will support your foot and ankle properly. You can purchase low-angle shoes, mid-ankle shoes, or high-tops. Each has an increasing level of ankle support. Your shoes need to be tight enough to be supportive, but if they are too tight, you could end up breaking one of the metatarsal bones in the foot while running up the court.

The best shoes tend to have an all-leather upper, but some synthetics and mesh-hybrid options are just as good for a cheaper price. You'll want secure lacing and non-skid, non-marking soles.

Some basketball shoes have these "air bubbles" or "springs" in the soles that are supposed to give your momentum more leverage. I've found that some are extremely helpful and others just break apart after a couple of practices. Since each foot is a little different, you'll want to consider all of your options here.

Step #2. Shorts.

Basketball is an aerobic game. You're going to run a lot. You're going to jump a lot. This means you will be sweating a lot. Now you don't need those short-shorts from generations past to be comfortable, but the best pair of basketball shorts shouldn't look like a pair of capris either. They should come to your knee, work around any braces you might need to wear, and stay up on your waist.

Trust me on this. Going up for a rebound while someone is tugging on your shorts will make you thankful for a secure pair.

Step #3. Equipment.

You'll need a good basketball in order to practice. If you want to work on your shooting skills and there isn't a local gym, then a basketball hoop, either permanent or portable, will be helpful. If you need to take a few basketballs with you to a practice, it's nice to have a bag for the equipment and a duffel bag for your clothing and miscellaneous gear.

Step#4. Joint Support.

There was this guy that I called "Big Hairy" in my college days that played at our rival school. His pony tail went down to his waist. His beard went down to his chest. He had so much chest hair that it literally popped out of his jersey shirt by the arm pit – like he had a chest hair pony tail. He was also nearly a foot taller than me. I went up to grab a rebound, he came in underneath me, and boom – twisted knee.

Joint support in basketball can keep you going when you're sore or carrying a lingering injury. The best knee supports may be useful as a proactive prevention as well. Leg sleeves, arm sleeves, kinesiology tape, and other items might also be useful to meet your specific physical needs.

Step #5: Warm Up the Correct Way

As with any aerobic sport or activity, you will want to warm up your muscles before you go 100% into the practice or game. A

20-minute warm-up period will stretch out the muscles a bit, get the joints looser, and help you get into the right mental state to play or practice.

Step #6: Start Jogging, Cycling, or Walking Every Day

Basketball is a very demanding sport. You can play it in any physical condition if you wish, but you'll have a better overall experience if your body can support your basketball activities. Even before you make it to your first basketball practice, you'll want to begin some exercise habits at home.

It is beneficial to run an average of 2 miles per day so your cardiovascular system is strong enough to support your physical efforts while playing basketball. You could also walk 3-4 miles if you prefer or take a 20-mile bicycle ride.

If your knees complain when the weather changes, it can be useful to make these at-home exercise be low impact. That way you can save the running for the court. Consider the ElliptiGO outdoor elliptical bike as an option to mix running and cycling together.

Step #7: Lay Off the Caffeine

My town was small enough that I got to work out and play with the varsity basketball team in the 7th grade. The first thing my coach told me was this: when you play basketball, you've got to stop drinking caffeinated beverages.

It's great advice. Because caffeine is a diuretic, your body will begin to purge its water resources prematurely as you play. This dehydrates you more quickly and that causes your brain to lose focus on your defensive duties or the ability to make a solid jump shot. You also crash right around halftime.

If you play basketball casually, give the caffeine a rest for a couple days before a game. Go with a vitamin pack instead so you can get moving in the morning if needed.

Step #8: Work on the Dribble

This is the one area of basketball practice I always wished I'd focused on more. Pretty much anyone can dribble with their dominant hand. It takes practice and dedication to work on a dribble with your weak hand.

A good place to start with this is to begin dribbling between each hand. One dribble with the right, then one dribble with the left, going back and forth as fast as you can. Once you begin to get comfortable with that feeling, begin running down the court (or the driveway, sidewalk, or street) using this alternating pattern.

Step #9: Work on Your Shot

Defense might win championships, but you need some sort of offense in order to win the game. It doesn't have to be pretty to be effective. My first varsity basketball game saw my team win 39-38. I scored 6 points. I think I took 25 shots.

Working on your shot should begin with a specific area on the court. Pick a spot which makes you feel comfortable. Then practice shooting from that exact spot for at least 15 minutes every day. Over the first few days, you might miss a ton of shots. Don't give up. You're working on your hand/eye coordination here. Eventually those shots are going to go in.

Once you can consistently hit about 70% of your shots from your most comfortable position, go to the other side of the court in the exact same spot. This will help your mind be able to process the reverse angle more effective. Again – you might miss a few at first. You'll also find that it is easier to sink shots more effectively.

Step #10: Bring in the D

High school basketball has started to incorporate a shot-clock like college and the professional leagues do in some areas. This means you've got to be able to think on your feet, read the game, and predict where the ball is going to be.

In that 39-38 game that I won, a guy on the other team shot a long three-point shot that looked a bit short to me. As everyone gathered around the hoop to rebound the shot, I moved backward. Sure enough, the rebound came long and I was in a position to grab it and put in an uncontested layup.

Defense in basketball isn't necessarily about watching the ball. It's about watching the shooting mechanics of the player you're defending. You watch their hips instead of their feet. This will stop your ankles from being broken on a good move so you can still be in a position to defend. Never reach for the basketball. Predict where it is going to be and then slap at it there.

Sometimes you'll hit the player and get a foul. If you read the game pretty well, you'll be getting the ball a lot or intercepting a pass fairly often.

And the most important thing to remember about defense is this: you're entitled to your position on the court once it has been established. This includes any space that exists above you as well. The same is not true for the space beside you. Keep your hands straight up on the vertical. Jump straight up to defend. If there is contact between you and the offensive player, it's their foul if you've done a straight vertical. It's your foul if you are reaching.

Step #11: Make Sure to Have Fun

Basketball can be a lot of work. You are going to be exhausted. If you're running suicide drills consistently, your chest will feel like it wants to explode. The bottom line is this: when you are in better shape than your opposition, then you are in a better position to win.

Focusing on your dribbling, defense, and shooting can even feel boring at times, especially when you keep doing the same thing over and over again. It's that repetition that will make you better. You shouldn't have to think about making a 10-foot shot. You should just be able to do it.

The same is true for your defensive drills. You shouldn't have to think about what position you need to be in to stop the ball. Just be there.

All of this work can be very draining. Sometimes it will not seem like much fun. If you can find ways to keep having fun in the midst of that pain, however, you will be that much closer to experiencing a win.

Are You Ready to Begin Playing Basketball?

This beginner's guide to basketball is intended to get you up and running for the first time. Basketball requires a complete set of skills that includes working with a team. You need to know what they can do and they need to know what you can do. The only way this knowledge can be learned is by working together. By being committed to one another.

Chapter 8: Basketball & Nba Betting
FOR BEGINNER

Even if you've never bet on any sport in your life, you've no doubt watch the fast-paced action of pro basketball NBA games. Perhaps you've watched people play basketball in the park and wondered how betting on this exciting sport really works?

According to sports betting experts, basketball NBA is second only to soccer in popularity all over the world. Consequently, there are thousands of highly lucrative betting markets available from leading sports betting websites. Virtually all of the sports betting providers that we recommend feature the hottest basketball betting action available.

Find out how you can start betting on basketball as well as on the NBA (National Basketball Association) today with our full guide to basketball betting. Learn how to incorporate the most effective and most popular basketball betting strategies to maximise your wins, right now!

Basketball & NBA Betting Breakdown

Basketball is a high-paced and fast-moving sport where virtually anything can happen on the day. Points are scored at high speed, and basketball NBA teams can rack up huge scores very quickly. These and other factors make it ideal for sports bettors that enjoy a challenging and dynamic betting environment, especially if live betting markets are preferred.

Lebron James Lakers NBA

Basketball is played all over the world and there are many leagues worth betting on in Europe, Asia, Africa and the Americas. The United States especially, with its renowned NBA basketball league is arguably the best of the best.

Getting into basketball betting is very easy to do and, with just a little bit of knowledge regarding the best betting strategies for basketball, you can make substantial profits. Whether you choose to get your feet wet with college basketball leagues from around the world, or you prefer diving into major league basketball, we break down the most essential basketball bets and sports strategies right here.

Over/Under Bets – Accuracy on the Basket Counts on the Day

If you've ever watched an intense basketball game, you may have been surprised to see just how many points can get racked up by both teams during the game. Basketball NBA scores can sky rocket very quickly, which makes it the ideal game for the over/under betting option.

Basketball is a game where defence and offence are of equal value. After all, your team can be great at offence, attacking their opponent's basket relentlessly but, if their defence is weak, they will be vulnerable to counter attack and still lose on the day.

With so much dynamic interplay involved in the game of basketball, making the call for an outright winner can often be very difficult. However, the ebb and flow of points scored can often be ideal for predicting whether a given game will end over a certain total or be under it.

This is why you will often find the over/under betting option in every serious basketball bettor's betting strategy. The flexibility of the over – under bet means that, if two defensive teams are competing, the low scoring game can be covered. By the same token, two high scoring teams may push the final total over the given line, making the over bet a good option.

Betting Against the Favourites in the First Quarter

Here's something interesting that is worth considering, and a sports strategy often favoured by those with experience.

In most sports where teams compete against each other, you'll inevitably have stronger teams and weaker teams, known in sports betting as favourites and underdogs. The same goes for basketball – with an exception.

Kawhi Leonard Raptors

Since the game of basketball is a game divided into four quarters, and their many games occurring over a season, coaches will often not start the game (first quarter) with their strongest players. A standard tactic is to save the best players for an appearance in the second quarter and, perhaps if needed, again in the fourth quarter, to help drive home the win.

This gives sports bettors the opportunity to try a very interesting option in basketball and NBA betting strategies, betting against the favourites in the first quarter. Since the favourites will more than likely not start with their strongest players, it gives the underdogs a chance to score early or pick up an early lead. This is a great strategy for quarter by quarter betting.

Looking at the Handicap – Underdogs or Favourite Picks?

Handicap betting is becoming more and more popular in basketball as teams from the bottom of the table go head to head with teams at the top. Weaker teams need all the help they can get, and bookies will give them a starting points advantage as the underdogs. Conversely, favourites will start with a handicap but with higher odds as a trade-off.

IS BASKETBALL GOOD FOR LIVE BETTING?

Absolutely! Basketball & NBA is one of the most dynamic of all competitive sports. A lot can change within a single quarter, which makes basketball one of the most exciting sports to bet on live. Take advantage of unfolding events by using a solid basketball betting strategy such as the elements described in this guide.

WHAT ARE THE BEST BASKETBALL BETTING OPTIONS TO GO WITH?

It all depends on what aspect of the game you are focusing on. The betting options covered in our basketball betting guide cover a lot of ground and can be adapted to almost any basketball game. Over/Under bets, handicaps and point spreads are just a few of the great basketball options available at most good sports betting sites.

College Basketball Betting Strategy Guide

Every year, college basketball season offers some of the best betting action on the market. However, there are now over 350 NCAA Division I teams across over 30 conferences. Finding a way to deal with the overwhelming volume of games and teams to handicap is perhaps the biggest challenge to anyone who wants to bet college hoops for consistent profit.

Thankfully, we're here to help. Our ultimate betting strategy guide comes directly from experts who have put their money where their mouths are and have made their livelihood as advantage bettors for years. Below, we give you the strategies and tips you need to become a consistently profitable college basketball bettor. Whether you're a recreational gambler looking for a few helpful tips or an aspiring professional handicapper, we guarantee that you'll find our tips useful.

Don't just wing it; you're playing right into the bookmaker's hands. Get knowledgeable with our help, and stay ahead of the books for the rest of your long and prosperous betting career.

Our guide is broken down into sections to help make things easy to find if you ever need to come back and get a refresher on a particular topic. Good to go? Let's get started.

I. Betting on Your Terms

Before you even get to your first bets, it's paramount that you lay the foundation for betting success with preparation. Over the long term, this is the biggest difference between winning and losing players, and the number one factor that separates the pros from the casual gamblers.

Some of the tips in this section are sports betting disciplines that can be applied to many other forms of sports betting as well. They are listed here because of how they help tackle the unique challenges that are specific to betting college hoops.

Make a Plan

The first thing you should do when betting college hoops is to make a plan of how you want to bet it. Will you be betting straight up or are you interested in parlays? Are you betting just spreads or are you betting money lines? How about game totals (or half totals)? Maybe you'll be betting all of these things?

Finding out what you want to bet is the first step in organizing your betting system, and we highly recommend that you do this first. Again, you can do this for any sport, but this step is more important in the college hoops industry when taking into account just how many games are on the board in one night.

Once you know what you want to bet, make sure to follow this next crucial step:

Keep Records!

No matter what sport you're betting, keeping records is a great habit to get into. Records help you stay disciplined within your system, and they can play a great quality-control role for you and keep your betting from going off the rails.

In college basketball specifically, keeping records is one of the most important things you'll need to do if you want to bet the game consistently and over a long period of time. In fact, many of the best minds in the college hoops business think that record keeping is the name of the game.

We agree wholeheartedly—Here's why:

1. Filter the Good Information from the Bad.

Unlike any other major sport to bet on out there, college basketball is a constant exercise in information overload. There is a huge volume of games almost every night, and for every game, there are tons of sports betting sites making predictions and lines based on all sorts of home-brewed algorithms and formulas.

There is so much information and data out there that it's overwhelming at times, even to seasoned gamblers. From our experience, all this information is actually blessing, but only if you filter and manage it properly.

2. Keep Yourself Accountable

At the end of the day, it's your money that's won or lost, so the ultimate responsibility to be accountable lies with you. If you trusted a poor system and it cost you some, hey it happens—but now is the time to use some tools and shore up your game.

Record keeping will help you combat your own betting biases, and over the long-haul will help you analyze which betting habits are strong for you, and which ones are costing you money.

For this tip, the best advice we have is to do what works best for you. For some, a simple spreadsheet with a few betting trends and a notes section is all you need. Some folks like to go more advanced. Whatever you prefer, just be sure that you do SOMETHING to track this. If you do, your bankroll will find itself on the upswing more often than it will when you're betting blind.

II.) Information is King

No sports bettor wants to hear this, but the truth is that we can't actually predict the future. There are folks out there who run so hot for so long that it can appear that way. What's the difference between those who break even at best and those who make a fortune year after year betting sports? One word:

INFORMATION

Data, records, memory, insight, gut – call it whatever you want. Just know that it's all information, and it's the name of the game.

Why Information is So Important

In a nutshell, better information will make you more money. How it does so shows you how important it is to stay on top of the sport you're betting. Here are just a few reasons that information is so important in college hoops betting:

Good Information Makes Money, but Staying Informed SAVES Money

You check the board and see two good and evenly matched teams facing each other. One team is a huge favorite, and you can't believe it! You rush a big bet in thinking you're stealing money, only to tune in and find out that the team you bet is missing one or two of their best players that day. The game's already started so you can't get out, and you watch as your money goes up in flames. Sadness.

This could've been avoided. All you had to do was find the injury report.

The example above sounds really basic, and most would chalk something like that up to common sense, but it happens all the time in sports betting. This is especially true of college hoops, where one injury is all it takes to get a line moving big time.

Chapter 9: Gathering Information

Now that you know how to avoid giving away free bets, it's time to put your knowledge to use and start making money.

This section will give you a basic strategy for information gathering on your college hoops bets. You can apply a lot of this information across any betting platform (and we encourage you to do so), but we've included the tips that best suit college basketball betting strategies.

In our experience, you only need to do two things to gather expert information on college basketball. The best part is that you can have lots of fun while you do it.

#1 – Watch the Games!

Watch the games and become more knowledgeable about the teams and players. Use the knowledge to make informed bets and make money while you have fun watching sports. That's the whole point, isn't it? YES! Good times!

All the fun aside, it's important to watch games. It' not enough to just look at numbers sheets. The very best gamblers have great betting instincts that they hone by watching the games. When you do so, you can find out not only just how many points per game a player is producing, but how he produces it. You find out where people excel and where they struggle. You get an education on the immeasurable. You get the FEEL of it all.

TOP TIP: RE-AIRS

One great tip we suggest is to watch re-airs of games whenever you can. There are too many games to watch in college basketball in order to get all the info you want, but watching select replays of games can give you precise information on a player or team that proves to be extremely valuable down the line.

With re-airs, you can get important question answered in a short amount time. How athletic is player X? Why did that top-ranked team get upset? How does player A or team B play when they're in foul trouble?

What questions you might want answered are up to you, but thanks to the wonderful Internet technology we have today, there are college basketball re-airs to be had everywhere.

From a betting perspective, we'd like to think of those games as our own personal library of betting information. Even the bookmakers and the experts have short memories from time to time, and you can get a leg up on them simply by having a longer memory than they do or caring to look for specific details in the games themselves.

#2 – Grab Data from Trusted Resources

There are a lot of ratings systems sites out there, like KenPom or TeamRankings. Each site has their own algorithm, and each system has its flaws. But they all have one thing you badly need: FREE DATA.

Don't fall behind. Get this information. It's extremely unlikely that you can be a consistent winner betting college hoops without using it in some minimum fashion.

Using Your Information to Make Winning Plays

Now that you're gathering this college hoops knowledge from all over, are you wondering how to use it? We've got you covered! Just read on for some tips on how to apply all your knowledge to maximum effect in the betting arena.

Find Trends to Exploit

This takes a bit of effort on your part, but it's easier than you think. In fact, you're already doing it to some degree whenever you bet. When you make a sports bet, you're telling the bookmaker that they got something wrong and that you're willing to risk to make them pay for it. This is the exact same concept, just with a bit more information at your disposal, thanks to the Internet.

Finding trends doesn't have to be just about the teams or the players—it can be ANYTHING. It can be referees. It can be time zones. It can be home vs. road splits combined with some genius idea you just had. There is no rock you can't look under if you think it will make you money. The point is to find something that goes against the grain in a way that takes advantage of the betting industry's everyday habits.

The great thing about all the data we have today is that, now, you can become your own expert and make tons of money betting sports, if you have the time and guile to read between the numbers and find something the books and the stats geeks haven't.

Maybe it takes time and lots of game data to craft your system, or maybe your magic trend comes in a sudden flash of brilliance. But by golly, find something and run with it if you think you've found gold. You want to maximize your profits before the market corrects itself. If it never does, enjoy designing your money bin.

Filter and Organize Your Data

There's a lot of data out there, and it goes without saying that certain statistical factors are stronger than others for purposes of betting. You want to make sure that you're paying attention to the right stuff before making your bet. You also want to save time wherever you can and still get the data that's most important to you.

Another reason to filter your data is because no data is perfect. We already told you that no matter where you get your information from, it's going to be flawed in some way. To best analyze the information you're gathering, you'll want to see it perform against your betting expectations.

Once you find the holes in a certain system or algorithm, you can make more efficient use of it. Furthermore, you can start to fill in the gaps in their data (if possible) by making a more personalized betting sheet that fits you best.

Making your own spreadsheet or data file is a great way to filter all of the information you're getting from other sources. You can get all the data you need from expert sources while still narrowing things down and saving time. This goes hand-in-hand with the "Keep Records tip" earlier in this guide, but it's worth a lot of money over the long run, and it's certainly worth reinforcing to any serious bettor.

If you don't have time for that sort of thing, it's no problem; we simply recommend that you try to have some kind of personal system to filter your information, and make sure that you have a way to improve that system as your betting history evolves.

III.) Solid & Consistent College Basketball Betting Strategies

A great way to get consistent results that can steady your bankroll is to make sure you have a solid fundamental betting base to draw on. Every sport is different, so you want to make sure your strongest betting factors are tailored to the sport you're betting.

Here are the most consistent factors that we've found for betting college basketball:

Specialize in a Conference or Region

There's an old saying that if you chase two rabbits, you'll lose them both. Well if that's the case, how do you think you'll fare chasing 350 rabbits?

With so many teams and games in college basketball, it's impossible to follow them all by yourself and get information at the quality you need to make constantly winning bets. Amidst the daily chaos lies a significant betting edge—if you're willing to narrow your choices and specialize.

For example, let's say you have a favorite team, and that team is in the Big East conference. There are ten teams in that conference. Following your favorite team closely will often include following the other teams in the conference to see how they are faring in things like recruiting, coaching and how much talent they lose/retain each year. That's nine other teams that you already have built-in homework on. There's an edge there! Exploit it!

If you're following the teams in that conference regularly, more often than not, you're going to find a scenario where the betting line is ripe to be exploited. The books often use sites like KenPom and the Las Vegas Sports Consultants (aka "The Wise Men") to come up with their lines. The bottom line is this: they have to make lines based on where they think action will land. Sometimes, this means just cranking out the industry standard data-driven line. College basketball is largely driven by betting lines like these.

Having specialized knowledge gives you an edge over this kind of bookmaking. Maybe a key starter is playing, so many algorithms will simply slot him in as "healthy," but you know he's tweaked up and won't be at his best. Or maybe one team or player is playing with particularly high or low confidence for certain reasons.

Whatever the case may be, if you have solid info that makes you confidently say, "Hey, I like Site X, but their computers don't account for…," then you're probably looking at an opportunity to make money against standard lines. Specializing in a few conferences rather than trying to follow as many teams as possible will provide more instances of added value against standard lines. The book won't care because they'll have their line to get action on both sides, but you'll be the big winner on the day more frequently.

Keep your knowledge base compact, but expert. Information that beats the mass-produced data is how you crush betting college basketball. On that

Note.

National Sites Entertain. Local Sites Make You Money.

When we do our research, we value the local beat writers and bloggers who have in-depth insights about teams and conferences. Their knowledge is valuable and often lucrative. Make their knowledge your knowledge.

On the flip side, be very wary about what you read from the huge sports networks sites like ESPN, CBS or FOX. These sites are huge corporations, and their primary objective is traffic. That's it. Their articles are written to entertain you and keep you coming back, not to give you expert advice. That's not to say that the folks there don't follow sports or don't have good stuff to offer. Just be sure that you can sort out fact from fluff, be careful on which writers you trust and verify rumors or scandals that they come up with before letting it affect your bets.

Betting Your Favorite Team

Just about every sports-betting guide out there tells you to play it safe and never bet on games involving your favorite team. The logic is sound—bias for your team can lead to emotionally undisciplined, or even outright destructive, betting. They say to cut this out of your system, and you'll remove a big money-losing trap.

We respectfully disagree, though, with a catch or two.

Being a big fan of a team and betting on them isn't the cliché sucker bet that everyone makes it out to be. It can actually be one of the most profitable plays you'll make over time if you can be disciplined with it. The most important thing to practice when betting your own team is to be brutally honest with yourself about how you expect the team to perform against the bet. Some people simply can't do this (thus the common perception). If you're one of these folks, then stick with conventional betting wisdom and STAY AWAY.

But if you have the discipline to stay honest and not overvalue your beloved club, you can find a lot of lines to exploit. You'll know when a line is off versus when it's spot on and shouldn't be played. You'll not only know when to bet for your team, but when to make money betting against them. You'll be your own betting savant, specialized in one team (and maybe even those who play against them).

If you decide to go this route, we highly encourage that you keep records on betting your favorite team. If the results are going your way above your normal rate with other bets, you'll have a good indicator that what works for your favorite team can be incorporated into a wider betting system, if you have the time to gather the information you need before each bet.

Small Conference Specialization is Lucrative

The books will generally have lines out for nearly every major conference team, and most of the mid-major conference games as well, as these are the most popular teams with the biggest TV audiences and fan bases.

But from a betting perspective, popularity can be just as much of a burden as it is a boon. The major conferences have large sums of money regularly bet on them. There are teams of experts around the world studying the teams and games every day, including the bookmakers. As a result, easy lines are harder to come by, and when they come in decent, it might only be by a thin margin.

Small conference lines, however, offer huge edges if you have the knowledge to properly take advantage of them. Don't believe us? Go find some college hoops ATS stats. Every year there are a handful of teams that absolutely crush the ATS on the season. What do most of them have in common? They come from smaller conferences, where the big money simply pays less attention. There is a lot of money to be made in small conference betting.

But how do you take advantage of this edge? The best method is simple – specialize. Pick one or two conferences and get your information gathering hat on.

For starters, we suggest that you pick a conference whose games you can watch easily. That often means a conference whose games are on TV where you live, or who has regular Internet broadcast access. Like mentioned earlier, you'll want to be able to put a visual on the numbers you're seeing in stat sheets. You'll also want to get a feel for the intangibles, like home venues or coaching, which can play a big role in smaller conferences.

One of the big drawbacks of small conference betting is that lines are not always published every day like they are with the big conferences. This is especially true on weekends when college hoops betting markets have to compete with other sports such as football or a big boxing/MMA fight. The small conference market is way better today than it was a decade ago, and it keeps getting better every year, largely thanks to the Internet markets.

While there may be less everyday lines compared to the big schools, the good side of this is that when the lines are off, they're WAY off. If you have knowledge that you think will beat the book on a small conference game, you're probably right! Go get that money!

Find Value Betting Against the Public

Compared to the major professional sports, college basketball betting lines are significantly influenced by public perceptions. Any sharp bettor out there will tell you that wherever there's strong public tendency one way, there's a lot of money to be made going against it in the right spots.

Here are some of the most common tendencies to look for when analyzing your bets:

Chapter 10: Overvaluing Of The Most Popular Teams

When you think college basketball, what teams come to mind? Why, if you said Duke, UNC, Syracuse, UCLA, Michigan State or Kentucky, you're not alone. You're really not alone.

It's no secret that these are the biggest national brands in the college basketball industry right now. When the tournament concludes in April and everyone turns their attention elsewhere, these are generally the only schools that still get regular love and coverage from the national media outlets. As a result, lines are often wildly inflated in favor of these schools on a regular basis.

This is especially true in the beginning of the season when no one really knows how some hyped-up freshman will perform or when bettors finally throwing in their action in to start the season just throw it at the big name schools. It sounds dumb, but it happens year after year after year.

Instead of following the herd, take advantage of their habits. If a big name school is playing a solid club early in the year that doesn't get as much publicity, be ready to jump on a line that overvalues the popular brand.

For example, see a November line of Kentucky vs. Decent Club U. and the line is -18.5? There's a reason for that; it's called, 'there's a lot of dumb money out there saying "I ain't seen Decent Club on TV in a while. They must be no good. Big Blue by 20."' Please go win this money.

The books put the line that high knowing they'll get the action on both sides anyway. Decent club doesn't have to win; they just have to cover a ridiculous line. And that line is going to be there every single year thanks to casual fans not knowing any better (no pun intended). This time around, be on the sharp side, and get a nice payday for all the reading you put in during the offseason.

Big Major Team vs. Mid-Major/Small Conference Team

This kind of plays off of the last tip, just a bit more generally. Again, the public perception that's being leveraged here is that the small schools simply can't hang with the big boys. These huge lines are everywhere during the November and December non-conference games, where most of these small teams play the bigger schools on the road.

If you know a small club is sneaky good, or a big team is still figuring out its identity (maybe from lots of new, younger players), the cover value is definitely there in a big way. A great spot to exploit is when a small school with lots of seniors plays a big-time school that is young overall, or graduated its top players, but is still getting lots of offseason/early season hype.

The big thing with following this tip is to make sure you're doing your homework on where the value is before placing your bets. This is definitely an area of positive EV when you find the right games and matchups, but the books are smart; not all of these lines are as sweet as they appear. Just be sure you've done your due diligence before you bet, and you'll catch the book slipping up way more than they catch you.

IV. College Basketball Intangibles: The Winning Edge

College basketball is filled with magical moments (including that shining one at the end). There are highs, lows, court-storming upsets and chalky brackets. But when the money is on the line, do you believe it's all magic? Or is it just that certain something that's observable, but not perfectly measurable?

The intangible elements that make college basketball so fun to watch also make for some of the best betting trends and things to watch out for. The best part about the intangible stuff is that you can run fantastically well when you're in tune with what's going on.

The elite players in any sport or industry will tell you that it's all about how you perform on the margins, and we totally agree. We think that keeping a keen eye on certain intangibles can mean the difference between winning and losing, so we've listed some here.

Everyone has their own opinion or weight on these factors, and they're super fun to talk about with friends or other sports bettors. However you slice it, have fun and find your winning edge! (In no particular order)

Home Court Advantage

What sets college basketball apart from the other sports is the complete lack of consensus on what home court advantage is worth. We all agree that it's worth something, but the claims of advantage range from 3 to 6 points depending on who you ask. Four points is a massive range. By contrast, the big argument in NFL home-field advantage is whether home field is worth 3 or 3.5 points.

We're not here to make a specific claim on what the number should be in college basketball. On the contrary, we think that all of the folks along that huge spectrum are correct, and that's the point.

If you take one tip away from this section, let it be this: Stop paying attention to the national average.

Home court advantage experts agree that home court varies by school. But to this day, they measure it all wrong. They simply take the mean of all the numbers and spit out the national D1 average. This isn't bad math, but the number doesn't tell the whole story well enough to be trustworthy.

SIf you can find lists of home court advantage by school, that's a far better start. We don't think that any one model ever truly has (or will get) home court advantage perfectly right in college basketball. There are simply too many moving pieces, and they change every season.

We do think there is a way to get a major step ahead of the simple math that's out there. That's huge because the macro-level numbers are a big influencer in determining the eventual opening line. If you can outmaneuver the books just by crunching an extra number, you can make large gains on a consistent basis.

To stay ahead of the bookmakers on home-court advantage, make sure to understand the following:

HOME COURT ADVANTAGE CHANGES CONSTANTLY

It changes every year for every school. Schools change players and coaches every season. Again, there are simply too many moving parts. Last year's 4.5-point advantage could be 6 points this year and zero the next. Add the fact that these are college kids and you can see why using the national average number, whatever you think it might be, will be wrong more often than not.

Constantly changing home court advantage has countless reasons, and explaining it is probably pointless. Your best bet is to just observe as much as you can and get a feel for why a particular school's number is where it is.

The great thing about enlightening yourself on home court advantage in college hoops betting is that once you get into the habit of customizing your number, you'll be ahead of a lot of bookmakers that simply make their own in-house number and go. You'll start finding line shopping opportunities everywhere, and some lines just waiting to be crushed.

THE ROAD TEAM MATTERS TOO

Is a team really good at home, or did they just play teams that don't play well on the road? Whatever the answer may be, it's better to take a look at both sides of the coin rather than sell out to one side of the equation.

HOME COURT DIMINISHES LATE IN THE SEASON

The numbers back it up: there is a slight decline in home court advantage in the late season (between a half and a full point) compared to November/December games.

This one is probably the easiest home court factor to explain. All of those scared freshmen? Not so scared anymore. They've gone through a season's worth of road environments and travel. They might not be grizzled, but at a minimum, they're not doe-eyed out there as much as they were earlier in the season. Another reason is that teams are just more set in their ways, and the venue isn't going to change that as much anymore.

Again, notice how this tip is also about keeping an eye on the road team when determining your home court number.

Rivalry Games

Our general advice for betting rivalry games is this: the play depends on the rivalry. The big thing with rivalry games is to avoid overplaying a line by letting your emotions override your good betting habits. This can sound a bit perplexing when you consider that high emotions are the source of the betting value!

There are always some great rivalry bets out there, but the edge is in finding out which games to hammer, and which games to stay away from. For the most part, you want to go about your normal betting routine for rivalry games, but with a few filters to help you find the best targets.

WHO HAS HOME COURT?

This is the first question to ask yourself if you're betting a rivalry game. Rivalry games do enhance home court advantages, just not always. This begs the question: do you give the home team the standard home court edge, or do you give an extra point or two because they're playing a rival? We think the answer lies in the next tip.

HOW HEATED IS THE RIVALRY?

Duke/North Carolina or Kentucky/Louisville are always hyped up as a huge heated rivalry, but it's not enough to be one of the nationally known rivalries. If you want more reliable betting value, you want to know who hates who, and why.

That's not to say that these big games can't offer value; it's just that sometimes the blueblood teams are more used to big games, so they might not get super emotional for a rivalry game like other programs might be. If you want to find value plays for home teams, bad blood is a great indicator. Not only is it a natural motivator for the teams, but fan bases can also get more rabid in-game and help home court edges get even edgier.

How do you find bad blood? Pay less attention to media folks who are paid to hype stuff up and pay attention to what the players and coaches are saying about the upcoming game. Also, be aware of the stakes. Is there a revenge factor at play? Who won the last game, and how motivated is the losing club to avenge their loss?

Is the game for true in-state bragging rights, or is it just a rivalry born out of both teams being in the same conference and performing well? All things the same, we'll bet the bragging rights home team far more often.

Reading Schedules for Value

If you've ever predicted a club's win/loss record just by looking at their schedule, then you know what we're getting at here. As a season unfolds, schedules start to tell a story that can help you predict future game outcomes. Players and coaches are people too, and they're prone to habits that can be exploited on the betting boards if you stay in tune with what's going on. Here are some of our favorite schedule trends to look out for:

Travel Fatigue

They might be on TV, but these kids aren't pros; they're college students zipping all across the country playing ball. Most of the time, programs make an effort to schedule cupcakes following a big tournament far from home, but it doesn't always go that way. Conference play can also be brutal for a team if they've been given multiple road games in a row to deal with, or have to zigzag, alternating between home games and far-away opponents in short space.

The bottom line is that if you think a team is a bit beat up and they have a daunting schedule ahead of them, you might be looking at a nice value play, even if it's only for one game.

Trap Games

They happen all the time. A decent club is hosting a big-time ranked opponent on Saturday, and it's going to be a great game. All they have to do is get past an underdog on the Wednesday night road game and they're sailing smooth.

Welcome to the classic trap game.

Finding these games requires a good nose on your part. Big game coming up + road tilt vs. hungry opponent doesn't automatically mean a team will lose or fail to cover. You want to have a good idea of the pulse of the teams you're betting first, but the value is there if you smell a trap game and you catch the book sleeping on the opening line.

Chapter 11: Letdowns & Bounce-Back Games

Another great value bet can be teams coming off of a big win or crushing loss. For unranked underdogs, a huge overtime win at home over a ranked opponent is awesome! It can also be emotionally draining. How about that next game two days later? If the bookmakers or computer models take the big win and give a team too much credit, you can find great value in betting the letdown.

This also rings true for teams needing to respond to bad losses (or just adversity in general). We like to save these bets for teams with respected coaches who have a reputation for knowing how to motivate their players. If you think a team has what it takes to bounce back from a big loss, or is in desperation mode to save their season, you might want to give them a look—especially if the books are giving them little respect on the betting line.

ATS Stats are Unfound Gold

ATS = Against the Spread.

There is nothing wrong with a team getting lucky a couple of times or going on a good run. But when a team is something like 12-2-1 or 3-11 ATS midway through a season, it is a huge indicator that the odds experts simply don't have a handle on that team. In such a case, the race is on. Go watch replays, find out what they're missing and hammer them the next time they make the same mistake.

Better yet, use the ATS stats to find systemic flaws. Maybe you'll find that a bunch of imbalanced ATS stats are coming in from one small conference. There is nothing more beautiful than finding out early that the sports book can't find an accurate line for NEC or Big West games.

Basketball Drill Guide: 5 Drills to Improve Your Basic Skills

Succeeding in basketball requires the natural gift of coordination, speed, and leaping ability. Whether these skills come to you naturally or require great effort, basketball players can significantly improve their overall game on both ends of the court by incorporating these essential drills into their daily practice routine.

What Are Basketball Drills?

Basketball drills are exercises used by teams and individual players to improve their fundamental skills. Common among youth players and professional teams alike, basketball practice drills teach on-court skills such as dribbling and ball handling, footwork, shifting momentum to the opposite direction, passing, shooting with proper form, defensive movements, and offensive rotation.

Why Are Basketball Drills Important?

Basketball players of all skill levels can benefit from performing drills on their own or under the watch of a trained coaching staff. Basketball drills help improve hand-eye coordination, dribbling, passing techniques, muscle memory, speed, and conditioning. The best drills prepare players for in-game situations and challenge them to take their current skills to the next level.

5 Essential Basketball Drills

Here are some basketball drills to help you improve coordination, muscle memory, and speed.

Two-ball dribbling: Many players default to their dominant hand when dribbling. This excellent drill forces players to use both hands. Try alternating dribbles, where a player bounces the ball with their left hand, followed by a different ball in their right hand, going back and forth as they walk down the court. You can also assign uneven dribbles, where one ball bounces high and another bounces low.

Defensive lane slides: To play good defense without picking up a foul, players need to glide from one position to another. Whether you're a guard protecting the top of the key or a center in the paint, you'll want to work on your defensive slides. Work on mastering three key movements: side-to-side, front-to-back, and back-to-front. Make sure you can lead these movements equally well with your left foot and your right foot.

The Mikan: The Mikan and the Reverse Mikan are named for one of the NBA's original stars, George Mikan. The drill helps bigger players (like centers and power forwards) get a shot off smoothly when they're close to the basket. To do a Mikan drill, hold the ball above your shoulders, and alternate close-up layups while standing on one foot, going back and forth from one side of the basket to the other. Keep the ball high, which protects it from defenders.

Weave drills: Weave drills involve three to five players running up and down the basketball court, weaving in and out of each other's lanes, and passing the ball back and forth. The most common weave drills are the Half-Court 3-Man Weave, the Full-Court 3-Man Weave, and the Full-Court 5-Man Weave. Instead of running in a straight line, players weave back and forth to confuse defenders and open up space for passing. Although these complicated passing drills can be more successful with older players, youth basketball teams will also employ these drills to teach young players the fundamentals of passing in transition.

Transition drills: Spanning off from weave drills are advanced drills that guide players through transitions where there are more offensive players than defensive players. The 3-on-2 transition drill and 2-on-1 transition drill can teach players how to use a fast break to exploit an offensive mismatch.

What is the best material for a basketball?

Leather is the best material for a basketball. Leather basketballs are perfect for professional-level indoor games such as NBA, WNBA, and NCAA. Composite leather balls can be used for indoor and outdoor courts. On the other hand, Rubber and Nylon balls are the most durable and manufactured especially for outdoor courts.

What is the best basketball for outdoor use?

Spalding NBA Street is the best basketball for outdoor use because of its synthetic rubber cover and easy ball handling. The composite material makes the ball extremely durable even on the asphalt surface. Best of all, it has consistent bounce and best buy for the money.

What basketball has the best grip?

Spalding NBA Official Game Ball has the best grip. This ball is manufactured with full-grain leather provided by Horween®, deep wide channels provide an excellent grip on the ball. Best of all, the ball feels great over time as it gets used.

What Does Bonus Mean In College Basketball? | Full Guide

May 5, 2021 / Beginners-Guides / By Aaron

Whenever you hear the word 'bonus,' what comes to mind first? For most people, it's the idea of getting freebies, especially after a great performance. In basketball, bonus means otherwise as it refers to the event when a team reaches the maximum number of fouls in a quarter or half.

But what does a bonus mean in college basketball?

Bonus in college basketball has a similar meaning to professional basketball leagues like the NBA – It usually means that a team is in a state of fouling out. The main difference with College Basketball is that the National Collegiate Athletic Association (NCAA) imposes stricter bonus rules.

What are the details for bonuses in college basketball?

Also, what does a double bonus mean? How many fouls are needed before a team enters a bonus? Find out the answers to these questions (and more) as you continue reading the article.

Bonus Mean In College Basketball

Bonus, also called the bonus or penalty situation, means that a team is in a state of fouling out. As such, the offending team already accumulated the maximum number of allowable fouls on a quarter or half. If a team that is currently in bonus and a player gets a personal or technical foul, the violation will provide the opposing team with free throws. The number of free throws given depends on the foul.

What is a Double Bonus in Basketball?

Double Bonus in Basketball

A double bonus is quite rare in basketball, although it's not impossible to happen. This event takes place when a team has ten violations in a quarter or half. The opposing team will be given two free throws if the team with the double bonus receives another violation after the tenth.

However, the double bonus scenario only happens in NCAA basketball games and not in professional NBA matches. Additionally, the double bonus status also becomes active when the offending team commits its fourth foul during overtime.

What happens if a team has a double bonus status?

For example, it's overtime and Team A already accumulated four fouls during this period. Now, the team needs to play more carefully than before. Otherwise, they risk giving Team B free throws, which will give the opposing team a significant advantage.

What are the Bonus Rules in College Basketball?

Bonus Rules in College Basketball

The NCAA permits teams up to receive up to six fouls per half. In contrast, the International Basketball Federation (FIBA) and the NBA permit up to five fouls per quarter. After those violations, each subsequent foul will give the opposing team free throws.

In college basketball, if a player commits a non-shooting foul while his team is in bonus, the opposing team will be given two free throws. However, the attempt stops if the shooter misses the first shot. On the other hand, the player will enjoy making another attempt at the basket if he makes the first one. This scenario is called a 'one-on-one.'

Also, keep in mind that offensive fouls will still count towards the number of violations gained by teams. However, basketball league officials won't award players with free throws for offensive fouls made. Furthermore, technical fouls don't count as team fouls.

Are There Controversies with Bonus in Basketball?

Controversies with Bonus in Basketball

Controversy thrives in basketball, particularly when talking about the bonus status. However, two serious controversies changed the way how many basketball enthusiasts see this specific rule.

The first controversy takes place during the 1983 NCAA Division I Men's Basketball Tournament. In one particular game in the tournament because head coach Jim Valvano made headlines as his NC State team upset the Houston team in the finals.

The reason behind this dispute is because the head coach is known for his foul-for-profit strategy. In other words, he likes to lead his players into performing deeds that'll make opposing teams foul out. That way, those opposing teams will enter bonus quickly, resulting in free throws for Valvano's team.

At that time, the NCAA knew what was transpiring but didn't have the means to prevent the incidents. So the college sports league devised the double bonus. In turn, teams would think twice before using Valvano's strategy of using fouls for profit.

Next, there's the Hack-a-Shaq controversy, which is a strategy used in the NBA. Since the NBA doesn't use the double bonus rule, players would intentionally use fouls to their advantage. In turn, the player can receive a free throw.

Take note that it's not rare to see professional basketball players being bad free-throw shooters, such is the case of Shaquille O'Neal. Since players would 'hack' fouls to gain free throws, these instances gave birth to the name 'Hack-a-Shaq.'

The NBA didn't like that players are exploiting fouls for their gain. Therefore, in 2016, the league implemented new rules. One rule to note is that teams will now only have one foul to give during the last two minutes of any quarter. Before, teams can still receive violations throughout the entire match but will only receive one foul in the fourth quarter.

What is a Team Foul in Basketball?

Team fouls are the total number of violations accumulated for each basketball team in a quarter or half. This number resets after each quarter or half, depending on the league's official guidelines.

For example, Player A has one foul while Player B accrued two fouls. Also, take note that both players are on the same team. Therefore, both players' violations are summed up as three team fouls.

Basketball players and fans will know if a specific team enters a bonus when looking up at the digital scoreboard. Most modern scoreboards will now have the word 'Bonus' under each team. This word will light up if a team has that status.

Chapter 12: Improve Your Basketball I.Q.

The best way to do this is to play basketball directly. There are certain reads and reactions you must instinctively make as a player, and they are developed playing 5 on 5.

If you play on a team, then remember always to be coachable.

Especially if you start playing at a young age on organized teams. By the time you are a senior in high school, you will have had many different coaches. Your job as a player is to try and soak up as much knowledge from each coach as possible to become the best player you can be...and that truly, is the secret on how to get better at basketball.

Another thing you can do to improve your basketball I.Q. is to watch basketball.

Also, do a good job listening to what the commentators say. You can pick up some great advice from some great basketball minds doing that.

Finally, watch your position. If you are a power forward, then watch how and what the power forwards are doing in the game and what their main jobs are.

Basketball I.Q. is something that takes years to improve but could be the ultimate

factor in your success in this game. If you want to improve at this game, there are many different things you can do. The important thing is that you do them consistently over a long period (years). When it's all broken down these are the things you need to focus on:

Developing Basketball Intelligence

Basketball intelligence combines tactical understanding with game awareness and decision-making skills. It is the capacity to make the right decision given an individual situation and to execute the play. An intelligent player exhibits the qualities of an expert performer. He:

Characteristics of an Intelligent Player

The "Sports Cognition Framework" describes three elements needed for sports success:

1. Decision-Making Ability: knowing what to do

2. Motor Skill Competence: being physically able to do it

3. Positive Mental State: being motivated and confident to do it.

Developing Basketball Intelligence focuses on the first element, the decision-making skills.

To execute the skills, players need the ability, the confidence, and motivation;

the following outline contributes to the development of technical skills, confidence, and motivation. However, the primary focus is the elusive decision-making skills which often separate the elite performers from the average players. This does not dismiss the importance of ability, confidence or motivation, as the three elements work together in sports performance.

Basketball is a fast-paced game which requires players to make split-second decisions. Players who anticipate and make decisions faster than their opponents have a decided advantage, and those players who make quicker and more accurate decisions exhibit basketball intelligence. These players "exhibit superior anticipatory performance compared with less skilled performers…Skilled players made a decision approximately 140ms earlier than less experienced players did, thereby providing a considerable performance advantage.

Basketball tends to be a traditionalist sport; we believe players are born with court vision and a high basketball I.Q., so we ignore its development. Coaches and players at the highest levels believe in its innate quality and these beliefs filter through the development system, which emphasizes recruiting the talented player rather than developing these skills in the players on the current roster. I don't know where it comes from but either a player has it, or a player doesn't have it, NBA Hall of Fame inductee Rick Barry said. "I can teach you how to pass, but I can't teach you how to see. If I throw you a pass into that little hole in the defense – that to me is the one telling the thing that determines whether you're a natural player."

These skills can be taught and learned. Players can improve their anticipatory performance, presumably as a result of a more refined ability to pick up subtle cues and to ignore irrelevant sources of information. To develop basketball intelligence, players must develop perceptual skills, so they know what to read when to read it and how to respond to what they read. Therefore, you need to change your approach to skill development, as the traditional block practice, technical approach fails to enhance game intelligence.

A player's success in a match situation depends on his ability to read the defense, quickly make the appropriate decision and execute the play in the dynamic environment. There are no fixed conditions during a game. When the player learns the jab-and-crossover-step move in an isolated drill with constant coach feedback, he does not adjust to the defender's presence. In the game, with a defender present, the defender creates a new skill. The player cannot pre-determine the jab-and-crossover-step move; instead, he must adjust to the defender and the defender's reaction to the jab step. The ability to quickly and efficiently vary a previously learned skill is only possible when the player has been exposed to a systematic development of his intellectual capacity.

Developing basketball intelligence is more time consuming and a more complicated process than learning several set plays, a well-organized press break and a basic defensive scheme. However, everyone wants to be a player with basketball intelligence: a player who always seems to be in the right spot and make the right play. Typically, the players who possess the advanced decision-making skills and anticipation skills which characterize an intelligent player are the players who progress to the next level.

Some great coaches micromanage their players and do not attempt to develop their basketball intelligence. They run set to play after solid play and discourage players from thinking. If these coaches succeed at the highest levels, why should youth coaches spend time and energy developing basketball intelligence rather than skipping to technique development and performance?

Skills Development

Chris Paul possesses basketball intelligence. We characterize players as possessing a "high basketball I.Q." frequently, but what do we mean by this description? It means the game slows down for Paul, and he sees the play before it occurs. We use these expressions commonly, and we accept the notion that one player plays the game in slow motion while everyone moves at regular speed and that some players see into the future.

Expert performers are not endowed with superior visual function…perceptual and cognitive factors are better discriminators of skilled performance in adults. Experts typically exhibit more efficient search strategies…and are faster and more accurate at recognizing and recalling patterns of play from memory. When faced with a situation, a player with basketball intelligence recognizes and recalls the situation faster and more accurately than an average player which leads to faster and better decisions. In a game where every split-second matters, making faster decisions plays a significant role in a player's success.

Everyone has a limit to the amount of information he can process at one time.

Think of your brain as a camera that takes 40 pictures per second. In normal situations, your brain takes an equal number of pictures in each concentration area. However, if you shift your attention, you can take more pictures in the desired area. When we say that the game slows down for Chris Paul, we mean that Paul directs his attention appropriately; he shuts off his thoughts, so he takes 40 external pictures.

Therefore, he sees more. He sees important postural cues that other players miss because he concentrates appropriately at the right time.

Beyond using the correct attentional style at the right time, Paul ignores unimportant information and focuses on the most relevant information or cues. When penetrating with the basketball, he takes in the entire court; however, with his attention directed appropriately, he sees things that average players miss. When he sees these visual cues, like a defender shifting his weight or changing his stance, he combines them with his advanced search strategies based on his experience which helps him to anticipate the play. Because he anticipates, he sees the play before it occurs.

We think that we see a superior vision from an innately talented superstar. In reality, we see the results of basketball intelligence. Paul perceives and interprets information more efficiently and effectively, and his perceptual-cognitive advantage develops through specific adaptations that occur through extended engagement in the sport. If these skills develop through sports engagement, they are as much environmental as they are innate. Therefore, how can you develop these qualities? First, you must understand the skills that you hope to improve and the best way to develop those skills.

Block training leads to immediate improvement in practice performance. However, the immediate gains do not equal learning, as learning requires relatively permanent changes in performance and retention from one session to the next. Skill gains in practice might be the result of temporary factors. In a subsequent session or game, the temporary effects dissipate, leaving a lower performance level than during practice. Block training stores the information in short-term memory, which is why players forget how to use the screen at practice the next day.

Because players do the same thing over and over, their practice performance improves. However, they do not necessarily learn the skill.

Chapter 13: Improve Your Shooting

You don't have to be a great athlete to be a great shooter. You do have to have at least average coordination and strength. You can improve yourself in these areas. You must master the basic shooting fundamentals. There are always variances in what or how the fundamentals are taught, but most coaches teach the same basic things. The important thing is to master them. Many players are good shooters in practice and poor shooters in games. You must try to duplicate game conditions when you practice. That means shooting when you are tired, shooting under pressure, and shooting with distractions. Many players master the fundamentals, but can't relax or concentrate. Don't overlook working on these areas.

Once you have mastered the fundamentals, confidence becomes

crucial. The brain records every make and miss. Make sure you make a lot more than you miss. Plan your practices accordingly. A good rule is: if you miss 2 in a row, move in and don't move out until you make 3 in a row. Don't set yourself up for a bad shooting workout. Don't shoot after lifting weights or if your legs are too tired. To shoot well, your body has to be ready. If you are having the occasional bad day, then stop shooting and work on other areas of your game. You should never have a bad shooting workout. Leave every workout with the confidence that you are a good shooter.

Shooting Form and Technique

The following points are critical to developing your shot. It is important to concentrate on perfecting these basics before attempting to learn different types of shots.

Fingertip control – Do not let your palm touch the ball. The ball should be controlled by the fingertips at all times. This will help in controlling the direction and obtaining a good backspin.

Your shooting hand controls the ball – The opposite hand is used for balance, and control up until the release. Be sure that your opposite hand is on the side of the ball and not in the way of the flight of the ball.

Elbow Alignment – Your elbow (on the shooting arm) should be close to your body and lined up with the target. If your elbow moves out and away from your body it may change the direction of the flight of the ball.

Release-Follow through-Flip-Finger spread – The release of the ball should be with your wrist and not entirely with your arm. If you use your arm too much, you will have trouble controlling the distance of the ball. The final release should see the support hand drop off, and the shooting hand follows through with a flip of the wrist. The fingers should be spread, and the follow through should remain until the ball goes through the net.

Target – There are many different ideas on what you should look at when you shoot the ball. Here are three acceptable targets, depending on your shooting needs and desires.

Arc – It is important to have a good arc on the ball. This increases the chance of making the basket, by increasing the area of the target. A flat shot has to be a perfect shot to go in. If you have a flat shot, you can improve it by shooting over an artificial barrier to increase your arc (e.g. a friend with a broom). The best way to improve our arc is by learning to shoot for a swish.

Rotation – The ideal shot has a backspin to the ball. This backspin is what gives you the good touch on the ball. With good rotation, you increase the chances of getting a bounce up if the ball hits the rim. The rotation is created with the fingertip control and follows through. You can check your rotation by lining the seams of the ball perpendicular to your fingers and flipping the ball up to check the rotation.

Concentration – All the correct fundamentals are not enough if you do not have good concentration.

Shooting Form Drills

Form shooting (without a ball) – this drill is to evaluate your form. Take an imaginary shot and watch your form. Shoot in a mirror to check your elbow. Start the drill in slow motion to check all of your fundamentals.

Form shooting (with the ball) — This is also to evaluate your form. Shoot the ball straight up in the air. Watch the rotation of the ball. Watch your follow through. Do as many repetitions as needed to develop consistent fundamentals.

Flip drill — Stand right next to the basket and shoot with one hand. Do not use your legs. Concentrate on your form (especially the flip of the wrist and follow through). Work on getting your eyes on the target and shooting for a swish. Work your way around the basket, but stay close. Work on bank shots, too.

Important — Be sure that the ball comes down off the backboard when shooting a bank shot. Pick your spot on the board and be sure to keep your eyes on that spot. See how many you can make in a row. If you have a partner, make a competition out of the drill.

Jump Shot (Without The Dribble)

It is important to note that you should not attempt to shoot a jump shot until you have mastered the fundamentals, and you have developed enough physical strength to shoot the shot.

Incorporating your legs into the shot – The ideal jump shot is merely a normal fundamental shot with a jump added. The jump is to help you shoot over another player. The rest of the shot should remain the same.

Rhythm – The toughest thing about shooting the jump shot is the timing of the jump and getting your shooting motion to coordinate with the jump. The following are extremely important:

Distance – When you are learning the jump shot, start in very close and begin with a small comfortable jump. You should stay in close until you get your timing down, then slowly move your way out. NEVER SHOOT OUTSIDE OF YOUR RANGE. This will hurt your fundamental form, and confidence. As you increase your distance, let your legs do more work to help get the ball to the target. If you use your arms more to increase your range, you will give up accuracy and consistency.

Coming off picks – the important thing to remember in using a pick is to come off the pick carefully to lose the defender. The second thing is to guard against floating. Preparing for the shot – In coming off picks and in open court shooting, you need to prepare yourself for the shot as soon as you realize that you are open. When you know that the pass is coming, prepare your feet, body, and hands so that you are immediately prepared to go into your shot.

Jump Shot Drills

Spot Shooting – Make your pass (use a toss back, a wall, or a backspin bounce... if you have a partner, use one player as a rebounder-passer). Start in close and work your way around the basket. When you have become proficient at that distance, then move out 3 feet.

Position Shooting – Pick a spot (in close to start). Shoot from the same spot until you have made a certain %, then move.

Time Drills – Shoot for a minute from one spot, then move. Count the number of made shots in a minute.

Chair Drills – Use chairs or cones to simulate coming off a pick.

Follow The Leader – One player shoots the jump shot, then rebounds his shot and passes back to player #2 at the same spot. #1 then moves to another spot to receive the pass from #2 after he rebounds his shot.

Working On Footwork – Pick two shooting positions. #1 shoots from position 1. #2 rebounds and passes to #1 at position 2. Then continue back to position 1. Go for 30-60 sec. And rotate. Concentrate on preparing your feet and legs before you receive the pass.

Full Court Shooting – Using 2 or more baskets, #1 shoots, #2 rebounds and outlets to #1. #2 runs to the spot at the next basket. #1 dribbles to the middle and then passes to #2 for the shot.

Jump Shot (With the Dribble)

Shooting with the dribble involves a lot more skill and balance, but once you learn the technique of moving the dribble into the shot, the rest is the same.

Using the dribble as a take-off for your jump shot – At first, you will need to come to a balanced stop, collect yourself, and then take your shot. As you develop your skill, you should make the dribble a part of the shot. As the ball comes off the floor, it should go right into your shot preparation. The last dribble before you shoot should be a harder dribble, to help get into the shot quicker. Once you master this, your release will be much more rapid.

Protecting the ball – One common fault that players have is showing the ball too much when shooting off the dribble. The ball must be brought up on the side of the body to protect it from the defender. After you have cleared the defender, then you adjust it to go into your shot. It is especially difficult to line up your shooting elbow when shooting off the dribble (even harder when dribbling with the shooting hand).

Taking the dribble to the basket – It is to your advantage to take the dribble to the basket for a pull-up jumper. This will allow you to shoot closer, and get the defender off you. When you dribble laterally for the shot, you allow the defender to stay close, and you get no closer to the basket.

Open court dribble – When shooting off the dribble it is important to have your speed under control and gain balance before you attempt the shot. In the open court under a full speed dribble, you must learn at what speed you can stop and get off a controlled shot. You must also learn to get a rhythm with your dribble when you see the possibility of a shot.

Jump Shot Drills

Rhythm Dribble-Shot – Start in close. Dribble the ball in a stationary protected stance.

Work on establishing a rhythm with a three dribble-hard dribble and shot. Stay in close and work with the left and right dribble. Slowly work your way out.

Dribble Jumpers – position and spot – this is run the same as position and spot shooting except that you use one dribble before the shot. Be sure that the dribble is going to the basket.

Dribbling Off Picks – Same as above, except using a cone or chair for a pick. In this case, you may be using a lateral dribble for the shot.

Full Court Dribble Shooting – Using 2 or more baskets, you dribble to determined spots at each basket. Work on stopping at the spot and shooting under control. Increase the speed of the dribble as you improve.

Full Court Follow The Leader – Same as above, except with two people in the competition. If the leader misses and follower make, then the follower takes the lead.

www.ingramcontent.com/pod-product-compliance
Lightning Source LLC
Chambersburg PA
CBHW070554010526
44118CB00012B/1315